WITHDRAWN

ELIZABETH I
AND THE RELIGIOUS SETTLEMENT
OF 1559

ELIZABETH I
AND THE
RELIGIOUS SETTLEMENT
OF 1559

BY

CARL S. MEYER

CONCORDIA PUBLISHING HOUSE

SAINT LOUIS

Concordia Publishing House, Saint Louis 18, Missouri
Concordia Publishing House, Ltd., London, W. C. 1
Copyright 1960 by Concordia Publishing House
Library of Congress Catalog Card No. 60-11413

Manufactured in the United States of America

To
Lucille

PREFACE

The four-hundredth anniversary of the Elizabethan Religious Settlement provides the occasion for this monograph. The changes and compromises of 1559 in the religious affairs of England have influenced the whole course of English history during the four hundred intervening years. If the official religion of England had been Roman Catholic and the Puritan party had grown up under a mild regime, ruthless suppression or revolution would have been the outcome, and the religious struggle in France might have been paralleled. Had the Elizabethan religious struggle been more radical, the character and outlook of the entire nation would have been different. The consequences of this settlement, therefore, make it worthwhile to study the settlement itself.

The settlement is worth studying also for its own sake. The story of that settlement is here isolated — total isolation is impossible — from the previous changes under Henry VIII and Edward VI. The Elizabethan Settlement, however, in this study is not contingent on them. The purpose of this book is to present the events of 1559 which culminated in the Elizabethan Settlement.

The Parliament of that year was the legal agency by which this settlement was brought about. The analysis of the actions of Parliament demonstrates that the Religious Settlement was not simply an act of Tudor absolutism. It demonstrates, too, that the settlement was in part political. Religion and politics were not divorced in the sixteenth century — nor were religion and life.

The sixteenth century was greatly interested in theological problems, much more so than is the twentieth century. A resurgence of theological concerns, demanding a return to tenets and beliefs of the sixteenth century, pervades the ecclesiastical scene today. For both reasons the treatment of the Elizabethan Religious Settlement as here presented has concentrated heavily on theological problems.

In that concentration other aspects of the Elizabethan Settlement could not be neglected. The reception which the settlement received was not uniform. The adherents of the Old Religion persisted. The radical Protestants, especially among that vociferous group returning from exile, grew in strength. Nationalism furthered the favorable reception of the Elizabethan Settlement.

This account of the settlement is not an exposition of the church or religious affairs in the reign of Elizabeth. The narrative, nevertheless, shows the immediate ramifications of the settlement.

A book such as this owes much to many people. Permission to quote has been given by the St. Martin's Press, The Macmillan Co., and Alfred A. Knopf, all of New York, and Macmillan & Co., Ltd. of London. To the authors and editors whose works are acknowledged and listed, publishers and librarians, critics, and friends, to all of these, known and unknown, the author is grateful. His wife, to whom the work is dedicated, merits a special word of thanks.

15 May 1959   CARL S. MEYER

CONTENTS

ELIZABETH I
AND THE RELIGIOUS SETTLEMENT
OF 1559

CHAPTER I

"GOD SAVE THE QUEEN"

loody Mary" died on 17 Nov. 1558. "The same day, at afternoon," a contemporary noted, "all the churches in London did ring, and at night did make bonfires and set tables in the street, and did eat and drink and make merry for the new queen Elizabeth, queen Mary's sister." [1] Elizabeth was the second daughter of Henry VIII. She was also the third of his children to ascend the throne of England, won on Bosworth Field in 1485 by the first of the Tudors, Henry VII. "I pray God save her Grace, long to reign over us, to the glory of God. Amen." [2] So wrote the clerk of the House of Commons on that day, and many concurred in that prayer.

Elizabeth was to rival, if not surpass, her grandfather in astuteness and competence as a ruler. No one, on the day of her birth, 7 Sept. 1533, could foresee the development of her regal stature. In the opinion of most of the courtiers and officials of the realm, a male child would have been more welcome. When she was baptized, Thomas Cranmer, the archbishop of Canterbury, was her godfather; the Duchess of Norfolk and the Marchioness of Dorset were her godmothers. Before Elizabeth was three years old her mother

[1] John Gough Nichols, ed., *The Diary of Henry Machyn, Citizen and Merchant-Taylor of London, from A.D. 1550 to A.D. 1563* (London: The Camden Society [Vol. 42], 1848), p. 178. Cited as *Machyn's Diary.*

[2] *Journals of the House of Commons* from November the 8th 1547, in the First Year of the Reign of King Edward the Sixth, to March the 2d 1628 in the Fourth Year of the Reign of King Charles the First (Printed by Order of the House of Commons), p. 52. Cited as *C. J.,* I.

was executed for adultery; Elizabeth never knew whether her mother or her father had committed the greater sin. By these events the status of Elizabeth was altered from that of a princess to that of a baseborn bastard. She did not lose the love of her father because of all of this, at least not such love as Henry might give her. "It is not easy to write that Prince's history, of whom no one thing may constantly be affirmed. . . . It is impossible to draw his picture well who hath several countenances." [3] His feelings toward Elizabeth fluctuated. Elizabeth, however, honored her father and at times identified herself with him.

As an adolescent she was shaken by a personal experience which had a far-reaching effect on her entire life. Thomas Seymour, her brother Edward's uncle, had married her father's widow, Catherine Parr. Elizabeth was a member of the Queen Dowager's household. Indiscretions occurred between Seymour and Elizabeth in the propinquity of this household. Elizabeth protested her purity, even as her mother had asserted her innocency. It is likely that both were telling the truth. Elizabeth never married, perhaps because of Seymour. As one of her biographers remarked, "In a sense the Princess was married to his ghost." [4]

Seymour's execution was ordered in 1549 by a Bill of Attainder passed by Parliament. In the previous year, Catherine dismissed Elizabeth from her household on account of Seymour's conduct. Seymour's downfall came about as a result of political plots, not because of his conduct with Elizabeth. She was not very deeply

[3] Edward Lord Herbert of Cherbury, *The Life and Reign of King Henry VIII. together with a General History of those Times* (London, 1740), p. 3.

[4] Katherine Anthony, *Queen Elizabeth* (New York: Alfred A. Knopf, 1929), p. 53.
See also Elizabeth Jenkins, *Elizabeth the Great* (New York: Coward-McCann, Inc., 1959), pp. 25 ff.
A. F. Pollard, *The History of England from the Accession of Edward VI to the Death of Elizabeth (1547—1603),* Vol. VI of *The Political History of England* ed. by William Hunt and Reginald L. Poole (Fourth impression; London: Longmans, Green and Co., 1919), p. 177 refers to Seymour's "improprieties" and affection with which Elizabeth regarded his memory. Cited as Pollard, *Political History (1547—1603).*

4

involved in any of these plots. However, already in her teens she was being educated in the labyrinthine ways of court politics. She never forgot these lessons.

There were other learning experiences before these. Her father had been a Maecenas to the humanists and with Anne Boleyn a patron of the New Learning. The Oxford Reformers spread Renaissance ideas in England; Sir Thomas More had been greatly concerned about the education of his daughters. The daughters of the king, too, received training in Latin and Greek. While serving as tutor to Mary, Juan Luis Vives, the Spanish humanist, had drawn up his "Plan of Studies for Girls." Roger Ascham, the great English schoolman, and William Grindall, his pupil, were the tutors of Elizabeth.[5] Grindall and Ascham furthered her proficiency in Latin and literature; she also learned modern languages — French, Italian, and Spanish. Ascham taught her to read classical Greek authors and the Greek New Testament.

All this was simply a part of her education. Her era did not know a distinction between "secular" and "religious" education. The religious emphases differed, especially when Protestantism was new to England and regarded as part and parcel of the New Learning. Elizabeth read Melanchthon's *Loci communes* with Roger Ascham.[6] This, however, was not her first introduction to Lutheranism. Her mother, Anne Boleyn, so the Spanish ambassador reported, was a Lutheran, using the label in a loose way as a term of reproach.[7] ". . . yet I know her for a spleeny Lutheran," Shake-

[5] John Nichols, *The Progresses and Public Processions of Queen Elizabeth* (London, 1823), I, ix, and x, cites Ascham and others about Elizabeth's learning.

[6] J. E. Neale, *Queen Elizabeth* (New York: Harcourt, Brace & Co., 1934), 16.

[7] *Letters and Papers, Foreign and Domestic, of the Reign of Henry VIII,* arranged and catalogued by J. S. Brewer and James Gairdner (London, 1862 ff), V, 148, Chapuys to Charles V, London, 22 March 1531. He refers to Anne Boleyn and her father, "who are more Lutheran than Luther himself."
Calendar of State Papers, Spanish, ed. Pascual de Gayagos (London, 1862 ff), IV, ii, 1531—33, No. 1047, 547, ". . . the Lady and her father, both of whom are staunch Lutherans." So Chapuys. Cf. also *L. and P.,* VI, 142 (p. 64).

speare has Wolsey say of Anne.[8] Elizabeth's mother, however, had little influence on her religious education. Very likely Elizabeth used John Marshall's *Primers;* that of 1534, for instance, had drawn on Luther's *Betbuechlein.*[9] Thomas Cranmer influenced her leanings toward Lutheranism during the first twenty years of her life. His loyalty to her father, his pastoral concerns for her mother, and his promise at her baptism compelled him to have a regard for her religious training. His friend Matthew Parker instructed her in religion as a child. Catherine Parr, with whom she lived during some of her most impressionable years, had leanings toward Protestantism, perhaps even toward Lutheranism. The acceleration of Protestantism during the reign of Edward VI came after her religious convictions had been shaped. The foreign divines, invited to England by Cranmer, a Bucer or a Martyr, had little direct influence on Elizabeth. Froude's judgment is correct: "Left to herself on her father's death, while the Anglican divines had developed into Calvinism, Elizabeth had inclined to Luther and the Augsburg Confession."[10]

The possible influence of Melanchthon's thought on Elizabeth needs emphasis. Melanchthon had dedicated the 1535 edition of his *Loci communes theologici* to Henry VIII. In that same year Thomas Starkey wrote his *Exhortation to Unity and Obedience,* "the first official statement of the English *via media.*"[11] Starkey took Melanchthon's teaching about the relationship between the natural law and *adiaphora* as the basis of his political science, "the direct ideological forbear of the Anglican policy."[12] Elizabeth

[8] Shakespeare, *Henry VIII,* III, ii, lines 98, 99.

[9] Charles C. Butterworth, "Martin Luther and the Marshall Primers," Appendix I (A), in *The English Primers (1529—1545), Their Publication and Connection with the English Bible and the Reformation in England* (Philadelphia: University of Pennsylvania Press, 1953), pp. 279 to 285; cf. pp. 59—67.

[10] James Anthony Froude, *History of England from the Fall of Wolsey to the Death of Elizabeth* (New York: Scribner, Armstrong, and Co., 1873), VII, 12.

[11] W. Gordon Zeeveld, *Foundations of Tudor Policy* (Cambridge: Harvard University Press, 1948), p. 128. Cited as *Tudor Foundations.*

[12] Ibid., p. 129. Cf. pp. 136—141; 144, 145.

6

knew both Melanchthon's and Starkey's works at first hand. In the 1520s lectures were given on Melanchthon at Cambridge.[13] The leading theologians of England in the 1550s knew his theology.[14] Through them Melanchthon's influence on Elizabeth was both direct and indirect. The parallel between the compromising attitude, the desire for unity, and the latitude allowed under adiaphorism by Melanchthon and Elizabeth was not accidental. Elizabeth had learned statecraft from Starkey with her Melanchthonian theology.

Her personal religious convictions were genuine and sincere. During the early months of the reign of Mary she kept away from the Roman rites restored by her sister. When she finally found it expedient to attend, she gave the impression of one who had not really surrendered her own convictions. She was not deeply religious, however. Some of her contemporaries were unsure about her religiosity, and some of her modern biographers have almost ignored it.[15]

Religion was not the only issue between Mary and Elizabeth. Mary feared that Elizabeth might become the focus of opposition to her. Her marriage to Philip of Spain caused a great deal of resentment among the people. Conspiracies were rife and rebellion brewing. When Wyatt's uprising was quashed, Elizabeth was not above suspicion of complicity, and she was taken to the Tower, a prisoner under taint of treason. However, she escaped condemnation. She was then quartered in the royal manor at Woodstock in Oxfordshire, with Sir Henry Bedingfield as custodian. Here she remained two years. Later she stayed at court with Mary at Greenwich for some months. Then she removed to Hatfield. The efforts to marry her off, as earlier, were unsuccessful. Elizabeth bided her time as heir to the throne, designated as such by the will of her father and an act of Parliament.

[13] H. C. Porter, *Reformation and Reaction in Tudor Cambridge* (Cambridge: The University Press, 1958), p. 84. Cited as *Tudor Cambridge.*

[14] Ibid., p. 338. Lowell Zuck, "The Influence of the Reformed Tradition on the Elizabethan Settlement," *Concordia Theological Monthly,* XXXI (April 1960), 215—226, stressed the Melanchthonian and Tigurine influences on Elizabeth.

[15] E. g., Jenkins, *Elizabeth the Great.* See fn. 4.

During the reign of Mary the fires of Smithfield were spreading terror and hatred in England. About three hundred Protestants were put to death because of their religious beliefs. The persecutions and the burnings, the presence of the Spaniards and the hope for the "good old days" of Henry VIII's reign, coupled with a growing tide of nationalism and a longing for stability, caused the average Englishman, at least in the southern and eastern areas, to hope for an early change in the monarchy and in the religion of England. Some 800 Englishmen had gone abroad. There they became more conversant with the Helvetic theology and more intense in their English patriotism. Among them was John Knox of Scotland, who blew his trumpet against the three women exercising royal power early in 1558: Mary of Lorraine as Queen Regent in Scotland, Mary Tudor as Queen of England, and Catherine de Medici in France.[16] He forgot, however, that Elizabeth, the hope of English Protestantism, was designated as the successor of Mary Tudor; nor could he know that she would succeed Mary before the year was out.

The five years of Mary's reign (1553—58) were the years in which Eliazbeth emerged as a mature woman. She was twenty-five when she was called to the throne. Her reddish-blond hair, set off by her lily-white skin and blazing blue eyes, was her crowning glory. In her bearing, when not given to outbursts of anger, she was regal. Her physical assets were surpassed by her mental endowments; these had been enhanced by careful training and by the buffeting to which she had been subjected. Her shrewdness and diplomatic skills, her astuteness and readiness to use womanly wiles, her insights into human nature and her ability to use human beings for her purposes had been perfected during these years. She was prepared to take her place as monarch of England. A German historian has said of her: "Masculine courage, royal self-conscious-

[16] John Knox, *The First blast of the trumpet against the monstrous regiment of women* ([Geneva: J. Crespin], 1558). Cf. A. W. Pollard & G. R. Redgrave, *A Short-Title Catalogue of Books Printed in England, Scotland, & Ireland and of English Books Printed Abroad, 1475—1640* (Lithograph reprint; London: The Bibliographical Society, 1956), No. 15070. Hereafter cited as *S.T.C.*

ness, and pride of country yielding to none, unfathomable cunning, too, when necessary, and skill in dissimulation that flouted all the rules of diplomacy — these were the characteristics of Elizabeth in the years when she was engaged in delivering the country from Spanish tutelage and in building up the Reformation." [17] An Austrian envoy at Elizabeth's court spoke of her "incredibly great prudence, great-mindedness and ability in all matters, and all her other heroic virtues." Then he added: "She is endowed with so many gifts of body and of mind, that she in no wise falls short of the most famous women of her rank and of her land." [18]

The most important single factor for her realm, however, was her religion. What *were* her religious convictions? We are told that Elizabeth complained because Mary doubted her loyalty to the Roman Catholic faith, adding "that she prayed God that the earth might open and swallow her alive, if she were not a true Roman Catholic." [19] Jane Dormer, who reported this, was a very devout Roman Catholic. Her conversation with Elizabeth may be true, but there is no additional proof of its accuracy. Perhaps Elizabeth was dissimulating. Edwin Sandys in Strassburg, at the end of December 1558, recorded a much more credible report of two members of the council. Mary had sent them to Elizabeth, he wrote, to tell her that Mary intended to settle the crown on her; she, in return, was to promise not to change the composition of the

[17] A. O. Meyer, *England and the Catholic Church under Queen Elizabeth,* translated from the German by J. R. McKie (London: Kegan Paul, Trench, Truebner & Co., Ltd., 1916), pp. 14 f.

[18] George, Count von Helffenstein and Gundlfingen to Ferdinand, Brussels, 16 March 1559, *Queen Elizabeth and Some Foreigners,* Being a series of hitherto unpublished letters from the archives of the Hapsburg family, ed. Victor von Klarwill (New York: Brentanos, 1928), p. 47.

[19] Quoted by Agnes Strickland, *Lives of the Queens of England from the Norman Conquest* (Stereotype reprint; London: George Bell & Sons, 1906), III, 98.
See also J. M. Stone, *The History of Mary I., Queen of England as Found in the Public Records, Despatches of Ambassadors, in Original Private Letters, and Other Contemporary Documents* (London: Sands and Co., 1901), p. 464, with reference to *The Life of Jane Dormer, Duchess of Feria,* p. 90.

Privy Council, nor to change the religion of the land, and to pay the debts which Mary had accumulated. As Sandys reports in verbatim fashion, Elizabeth replied:

> I am sorry to hear of the queen's illness; but there is no reason why I should thank her for her intention to give me the crown of this kingdom. For she has neither the power of bestowing it upon me, nor can I lawfully be deprived of it, since it is my peculiar and hereditary right. With respect to the council, I think myself as much at liberty to choose my own counsellors, as she was to choose her own. As to religion, I promise this much, that I will not change it, provided only it can be proved by the word of God, which shall be the only foundation and rule of my religion. And when, lastly, she requires the payment of her debts, she seems to me to require nothing more than what is just, and I will take care that they shall be paid, as far as may lie in my power.[20]

Various rumors, parading as precise information, were contradictory, and men believed what they wanted to believe.

Elizabeth, the Spanish ambassador felt, would not remain in the Church of Rome. Shortly before the death of Mary he reported: "I greatly fear that in religion she will not go right, as she seems inclined to favor men who are supposed to be heretics. And they tell me the ladies about her are all so." [21] Shortly after the death of Mary, another envoy was distressed because he saw that "by little and little" there was a return to the former "bad use." [22] The re-establishment of Roman Catholicism in England had been the

[20] Edwin Sandys to Henry Bullinger, Strasburgh, 20 December 1558, *The Zurich Letters, Comprising the Correspondence of Several English Bishops with Some of the Helvetian Reformers during the Early Part of the Reign of Queen Elizabeth,* edited for the Parker Society by Hastings Robinson (Cambridge: The University Press, 1842), Letter No. 2, pp. 3, 4. Hereafter cited as *Zurich Letters (1558—79),* I.

[21] Froude, *History of England,* VII, 13.

[22] *Calendar of State Papers and Manuscripts, Relating to English Affairs, Existing in the Archives and Collections of Venice, and in Other Libraries of Northern Italy,* ed. Rawdon Brown and G. C. Bentinek (London: Her Majesty's Stationery Office, 1890), VII (1558—80), No. 2, p. 2. Il Schifanoya to Ottaviano Vivaldino, London, 31 December 1558. Hereafter cited as *Ven. Cal.* VII (1558—80).

goal of Mary's existence; she had little reason to hope that her successor would retain the Old Religion.[23]

The doctrine of the Lord's Supper was the touchstone of Roman Catholicism and of Protestantism in that day. During the early weeks of her reign, Elizabeth continued to attend Mass. Mass was said at the funerals of Queen Mary and the Archbishop of Canterbury, Reginald Pole, who had died on the same day. Outward conformity to the rites of Rome was the immediate policy. On the doctrine of transubstantiation Elizabeth gave answer to the bishops in the substance, but not in the words, of the hymn stanza:

> Christ is the Word who spake it,
> He took the bread and brake it:
> And what His Word doth make it,
> That I believe and take it.[24]

Lutherans have taken this as a correct exposition of their doctrine of the Real Presence. Yet Elizabeth never called herself a Lutheran. The Prayer Book of 1549, more Lutheran than Calvinistic, was favored by her. She told the Roman Catholic ambassador from Spain that she favored the Augsburg Confession, the Lutheran confession of faith of 1530, or something else like it.[25] To him she

[23] Sir John Neale, "The Accession of Queen Elizabeth I," *Essays in Elizabethan History* (New York: St. Martin's Press, 1958), p. 46.

[24] Gwen John, *Queen Elizabeth* (Boston: Small Maynard & Co., 1924), p. 24.

This stanza is quoted also, among others, by A. L. Rouse, *The England of Elizabeth: The Structure of Society* (London: Macmillan & Co., Ltd., 1951), pp. 387, 388. That it is a proof of Elizabeth's "Laodiceanism" may well be doubted. An author who in making a passing reference to Luther, p. 470, cannot refrain from referring to him as "the loathsome Luther," is not the best of theological guides.

Nichols, *Progresses and Public Processions*, I, called this verse an "ingenious evasion of a captious theological question." Why not take it as a simple expression of faith?

Sir John Neale, "The Sayings of Queen Elizabeth," *Essays in Elizabethan History*, pp. 102, 103, disproves the Elizabethan authorship of these words.

[25] *Span. Cal. Elizabeth i.* 61—62 as quoted by J. E. Neale, *Elizabeth I and Her Parliaments, 1559—81* (New York: St. Martin's Press), p. 79; Froude, *History of England,* VII, 84. Neale's work will be cited as Neale, *E. & Parl.,* I.

11

affirmed her belief in the Real Presence in the Sacrament. Religion, she said, was a question of conscience, in which in life and death she meant to be constant. Perhaps she herself did not realize how close to the Lutheran views she was.

She was English. Creedal statements to which she might subscribe would have to advance the welfare of her realm. She proceeded cautiously, therefore, in her alterations of the religious practices of her country. She did not adopt the title "Defender of the Faith" immediately. An "et cetera" left men guessing. The security of the kingdom was more important to her than a rapid change in religion. Peace with Scotland and France came within half a year after her accession to the throne.[26] An embassy from the Lutheran king of Sweden, Gustavus Vasa, was treated courteously, but no commitments were made. The ambassador of Philip II, the Roman Catholic king of Spain, was likewise treated with respect. The king of Denmark, Christian III, along with Gustavus Vasa and the Protestant princes of Germany, received confidential but informal assurances that she was a follower of the Reformation and that she wished to be in close harmony with those who also were followers of the Reformation. In foreign as well as in domestic affairs she was intent on looking after the best interests of England.

During the coronation festivities one incident was regarded as especially significant. At the Little Conduit in the upper end of Cheapside a pageant was presented which portrayed Time leading Truth. Truth, dressed in white silk, carried a book in her hand, *Verbum veritatis,* the Bible in English. Elizabeth kissed the book and held it up with both hands. In her little speech of thanks she promised to often read the book. At Temple Bar a child spoke some verses, bidding the queen Godspeed.

[26] "A Proclamation declaring the Queen's Majesty's Purpoose to kepe Peace with France and Scotland; and to provide for the Suerty of hir Kingdomes, March 24, 1559," Samuel Haynes, ed. *A Collection of State Papers, Relating to Affairs in the Reign of King Henry VIII., King Edward VI., Queen Mary, and Queen Elizabeth, from the year 1542 to 1570, left by William Cecill, Lord Burghley* (London: William Bowyer, 1740), pp. 268—270.

Farewell! O worthy Queen! and as our hope is sure,
That into Error's place, thou wilt now Truth restore,
So trust we that thou wilt our Sovereign Queen endure
And loving Lady stand, from henceforth, evermore! [27]

She showed her clemency to prisoners detained for their Protestant beliefs. Two commissions, one appointed by Mary in 1556 against the Lollards and another appointed for the extirpation of heresy, were called to account. Persecution was revived later, but for the time being neither Romanists nor Protestants were to suffer for their beliefs. A foreign diplomat observed: "From the very beginning of her reign she has treated all religious questions with so much caution and incredible prudence that she seems both to protect the Catholic religion and at the same time not entirely to condemn or outwardly reject the new Reformation." To this observation he added the comment: "In my opinion, a very prudent action, intended to keep the adherents of both creeds in subjection, for the less she ruffles them at the beginning of her reign the more easily will she enthrall them later on." [28]

On Christmas Day Elizabeth walked out of her chapel after the reading of the holy Gospel because the bishop refused to omit the elevation of the host during the celebration of the Mass.[29]

Her proclamation on 27 Dec. 1558 forbade all preaching, Protestant and Papistic alike. Those who favored a change in religion were growing impatient, it was feared, because she was proceeding too cautiously. Disorders had taken place; images and statues had been destroyed. On the other hand, lewd words and epithets had

[27] "The passage of our most dread Sovereign Lady, Queen Elizabeth, through the City of London to Westminster, the day before her Coronation," A. F. Pollard, ed. *Tudor Tracts, 1532—88,* (Westminster: Archibald Constable and Co., Ltd., 1903), p. 391; cf. pp. 380—382; see also Nichols, *Progresses and Public Processions,* I, 38—60; *Ven. Cal.,* VII (1558 to 1580), No. 10, pp. 11—19, Il Schifanoya to the Castellan of Mantua, London, 23 January 1559; *Machyn's Diary,* pp. 186 f.

[28] Victor von Klarwill, ed. *Queen Elizabeth and Some Foreigners,* p. 47, George, Count von Helffenstein, Baron von Gundlfingen to Emperor Ferdinand, Brussels, 16 March 1559 [he had been in London before this].

[29] *Ven. Cal.,* VII (1558—80), No. 2, p. 2, Il Schifanoya to Ottaviano Vivaldino, London, 31 December 1558.

been bandied about. Decided opinions were being voiced in the pulpits. Now, the proclamation stated, nothing should be heard in the churches except the Epistle and the Gospel for the appointed day and the Ten Commandments. These were to be read in the vernacular. The litany used in the queen's chapel, the Lord's Prayer, and the Creed, too, were to be used in English without expositions or explanations.[30] Elizabeth wanted to set aside bitter disputations by this proclamation. The proclamation, however, was not obeyed by all. Some believed that they must preach "to the due honour of Almighty God, the increase of virtue and godliness," and for the "universal charity and concord" of the English realm. On the Continent it was reported:

> The queen has forbidden any person, whether papist or gospeller, to preach to the people. Some think the reason of this to be, that there was at that time only one minister of the word in London, namely, Bentham, whereas the number of papists was very considerable; others think that it is owing to the circumstance that, having heard only one public discourse of Bentham's, the people began to dispute among themselves about ceremonies, some declaring for Geneva, and some for Frankfort.[31]

Within weeks after this proclamation the coronation took place, on 15 Jan. 1559. The rites were in accord with the ancient usage. The oil of unction was applied; the Mass was said. More important, in the minds of many, the Epistle and the Gospel were read in English as well as in Latin. The coronation itself left the final answers about Elizabeth's religious convictions in some doubt. Oglethorpe, the bishop of Carlisle, performed the ceremony, the only bishop to participate in the rites. The archbishopric of Canter-

[30] Henry Gee and William J. Hardy, *Documents Illustrative of English Church History* (London: Macmillan and Co., Ltd., 1896), No. LXXVII, pp. 416, 417.
G. W. Prothero, ed. *Select Statutes and Other Constitutional Documents Illustrative of the Reigns of Elizabeth and James I,* 4th ed. (Oxford: The Clarendon Press, 1913 [1954 reprint]), 183, 184.
Ven. Cal., VII (1558—80), No. 2, pp. 3, 4 (Latin).

[31] John Jewel to Peter Martyr, Strasburgh, 26 January 1559, *Zurich Letters* (1558—79), I, 7, 8.

bury was vacant; Nicholas Heath was archbishop of York, but he refused to officiate, as did the other bishops. On the Sunday after the coronation the queen received Holy Communion according to the Protestant rite, *sub utraque,* under both kinds. On the following day, eight days after the coronation, her first Parliament convened.

Elizabeth's popularity had grown during these early months of her reign. The sentiment in her favor may be gathered from *An Harborovve for Faithfull and Trevve Svbiectes,* published in April 1559 by John Daye, in London. The author was John Aylmer. It was written to refute the arguments of John Knox in his tract against the rule of women, as the title said, *agaynst the late blowne Blaste, concerninge the Gouernmēt of VVemen, where he confuted all such reasons as a straunger of late made in that behalfe, with a briefe exhortation to Obedience.*[32] Aylmer reasoned that none can withstand God, who works in weakness. Queen Anne Boleyn had been God's instrument for retrieving the Gospel; "the crop and root was the Queen," he wrote.[33] The rule of women in a commonwealth, however, he pointed out, is not against nature; many countries have been well governed by women. Mary was deceived by churchmen; spiritual men should not meddle with politics. Scripture does not forbid the rule of women; a woman may rule as a magistrate and still obey as a wife. The Pauline injunction against the speaking of women in the churches applies, he argued, to public preaching, not to the secular rule of women. It is less dangerous, he continued, to be governed by a woman in England than anywhere else. Where mixed government exists, there the government of women cannot be dangerous. In England, he maintained, God has all the voices in His hands. The people must pray for the queen's estate and not dispute her right. The queen may oversee the church and still not be a priest. If it is argued that the government of women is more inconvenient than that of men, it must be remembered that heretofore England has taken greater loss by men's rule than by women's. After referring

[32] *S. T. C.,* No. 1005 (Harmsworth copy in the Folger Shakespeare Library, Washington, D. C.)

[33] Ibid., B 3, 2 verso.

to God's care, he discussed the need for obedience and voiced a patriotic appeal. "We be the Saxon's posterity," he pleaded.[34] England can be conquered by discord; her voice calls to her children: "Do you not hear how lamentably your natural mother, your country of England, calleth upon you for obedience saying, 'Oh, remember, my dear children, in what case you stand, your enemies be round about you. . . .' "[35] Religion and nationalism were coupled so closely in one instance that there is printed on the margin of one paragraph of this book, "God is English."[36] These words stand opposite the sentence: "He [God] would that out of my [England's] womb should come that servant of His, your brother, John Wyclif, who begat Hus, who begat Luther, who begat truth."[37]

Aylmer's supposition that the queen would marry was shared by all her subjects. Even her sister had taken a husband when she came to the throne; there seemed to be no reason why Elizabeth ought not do the same. The king of Spain, Philip II, her half-sister's widower, made overtures to her. The king of Sweden suggested his son, Eric, be considered; John Frederic, the Lutheran duke of Saxony, too, promoted his son as a candidate for Elizabeth's hand. There were royal princes in France; a royal scion of the Hapsburgs was a serious suitor. And then there were loyal Englishmen, nobles of the realm. Eric of Sweden sent his brother as envoy to Elizabeth in his behalf. The archduke of Austria, Charles, seemed to be favored for a while. But then there was Robert, Lord Dudley. Not a little gossip and even vicious scandal were attached to that relationship, for Robert was married, and the accidental or suicidal death of his wife gave added impetus to the tongues of the scandalmongers. Her first Parliament sent a delegation or a committee to her, asking her to marry. She assured the group, "I happily chose this kind of life in which I yet live." If she married, she would marry for the welfare of her

[34] Ibid.
[35] Ibid., R.
[36] Ibid., P. 3, 2 verso.
[37] Ibid., R. 1, i verso.

16

kingdom. "I will never in that matter conclude anything that shall be prejudicial in the realm, for the weal, good, and safety whereof I will never shun to spend my life." God might lead her to marry; if not, she said, "this shall be for me sufficient, that a marble stone shall declare that a Queen, having reigned such a time, lived and died a virgin." [38] In other Parliaments the marriage question was linked closely to the question of the succession to the throne. In other years, too, there were other suitors. There is no reason to doubt, no matter how flirtatious Elizabeth was, or how seriously she seemed to entertain the suits of foreign princes, or how tantalizingly she seemed to treat some of her courtiers, that in these matters, as in matters of religion, she acted for what she believed to be the best interests of her kingdom.

A much less vexing question had been settled at the beginning of her reign, the question of the Privy Council. The welfare of her country governed also her choice of her councillors.

She first appointed William Cecil her principal secretary and privy councillor on 20 Nov. 1558. He continued with her as secretary and then as lord treasurer until the day of his death, 8 Aug. 1598, almost forty years later. "Serve God by serving the Queen," he wrote his son shortly before his end.[39] In those words he summarized virtually the last half of his life. He had reached the age of thirty-eight on that day in Hatfield when Elizabeth solemnly told him: "I give you this charge that you shall be of my Privy Council and content to take pains for me and my realm." [40] Take pains he did. His grasp of details was as sure as was his insight into larger problems. Nothing seemed to escape him. He could relate the small and the insignificant to the great and important issues of the day. His advice to Elizabeth was as invaluable to her as was his loyalty. His integrity was unquestioned. In a position where others might have sought their own gain or might have used their office for the advancement of their friends

[38] Quoted from the British Museum Lansdowne MS. 94, fol. 29, by Neale, *E. & Parl.*, I, 49.

[39] Neale, *Queen Elizabeth,* p. 349.

[40] Froude, *History of England,* VII, 17.

17

and relatives, Cecil remained without the suspicion of corruption, even when Elizabeth created him Lord Burghley and appointed his son to the post he had held. His skill in diplomacy was surpassed by his patriotism, but always he took pains for his queen and her realm. He advised her on many occasions on many a question; she valued that advice even when she did not follow it — which was seldom. "Cecil alone possesses her confidence," the Spanish ambassador reported.[41] "Everywhere among the State papers of these years Cecil's pen is ever visible, Cecil's mind predominant," [42] Froude concluded from his diligent researches among those papers. Elizabeth's choice of Cecil was due to her extraordinary understanding of character and to a recognition of his extraordinary abilities.

Cecil's brother-in-law, Sir Nicholas Bacon, was made Lord Keeper of the Great Seal. Sir Nicholas gave the opening speech to the Parliament which brought about the Elizabethan Settlement. He was a moderate man who obviously favored Protestantism. Although he was an able man and a worthy councillor, he was overshadowed by the industry and ability of his brother-in-law.

Other recognizable Protestants appointed to the Privy Council were Sir Francis Knollys, Sir Thomas Parry, Sir Edward Rogers, the Earl of Bedford, and the Marquess of Northampton. None of them equaled Cecil, or even Bacon, in ability. Sir Francis Knollys has been called a Puritan. During the reign of Mary he had gone abroad because of his religious conviction. His Puritanism, however, was not of the fanatical kind. The Earl of Bedford, too, had been an exile during Mary's reign, but his religious zeal was not excessive.

Six of the men who had served as members of the council under Mary were allowed to withdraw or were removed. They were generally devout Romanists and personally attached to the de-

41 Ibid., VII, 187. The ambassador was Alvarez de Quadra, Bishop of Aquila.

42 Ibid., VII, 472. "William Cecil . . . was an administrator of the first class, as competent, as great indeed, as was ever Wolsey or Cromwell, and as honest as they were corrupt," said Philip Hughes, *The Reformation in England* (New York: The Macmillan Co., 1954), III, 4.

ceased queen. The most important among them was Lord Paget. His health was poor, and he was aging. Able and moderate, he would have been an asset to Elizabeth if his health had permitted him to serve on the council.

Nicholas Heath, archbishop of York, had been the Lord Chancellor under Mary. He could have retained this office, but he asked, as he wrote to Cecil years later, that he might be "utterly disburdened" of this office.[43] He had served Henry VIII loyally as court chaplain. He was a member of the commission that met with the German Lutherans in 1535 and 1536. Melanchthon had praised him highly. But Heath was not a Lutheran or a Melanchthonian, as his high position under Queen Mary testifies. Elizabeth possibly entertained the hope that he would declare himself for her and for England and for the change in religion. Before the year 1559 was out, Heath was deprived of his office as archbishop. Unlike Thomas Cranmer, whose writ for execution he had issued, he lived in retirement until his death in 1579.

Ten members of Mary's council retained their places in Elizabeth's council. Among them the Marquis of Winchester, the Lord Treasurer, was as moderate as were the rest. "His principle was loyalty to the family of Henry VIII; his creed, faith in God and English freedom, and hate of fanatics, [Roman] Catholic or Protestant."[44] The Earl of Pembroke was a military man, a power in the Welsh Marches, more in favor of Elizabeth than of Mary and happier now that he could serve her. The Earl of Arundel negated his usefulness. But there were others. Together they would advance the cause of the queen and of the country.

The duties of the council as a part of the administrative machinery of the government were not precisely defined. With the develop-

[43] Conyers Read, *Mr. Secretary Cecil and Queen Elizabeth* (New York: Alfred A. Knopf, 1955), p. 122 and p. 479, n. 9, with reference to British Museum, Cotton MSS, Vespasian F xiii, f. 297, letter dated 26 Sept. 1573: "I do remember that I did earnestly move you to stand by my friend and to be a mean to the Q. Majesty that now is, that I might be utterly disburdened of mine office."

Neale, *Essays in Elizabethan History*, p. 50.

[44] Froude, *History of England*, VII, 44.

19

ment of Parliament the Great Council's duties of rendering advice and counsel to the sovereign devolved on the more intimate group, the Privy Council. The Privy Council was not to be too large, although its precise number was not fixed. The membership of the council was not limited to the old titled families. With the changing complexities of society they might well be from the upper middle class. Elizabeth made good use of her Privy Council. At times it served as a sounding board for policies to be presented to Parliament; at other times it promoted the queen's policies, especially if not too popular, in either the House of Commons or the House of Lords. It kept in close touch with local officials in England, the justices of the peace and the sheriffs. It received the reports of diplomats who represented England abroad. The judicial functions of the council had been increased already under Henry VII. Branch councils had been established in Wales and in the North. Among all the members of the Privy Council none exceeded the secretary in influence or industry. But all of them had important duties. Foreign policy and the religious question were the chief matters with which Elizabeth's Privy Council dealt during the first weeks and months of her reign; these problems reoccurred throughout her reign.

These councillors were helping to build a modern state. The Privy Council was not yet the cabinet, but its duties in part paralleled those of the queen's cabinet today. The secretary, William Cecil, was not the prime minister, but his duties and activities closely coincided with many of those of a modern prime minister. England was no longer a feudal state, although some aspects of feudalism remained. It was not a Renaissance state, for the power politics of Machiavelli did not pervade it. It was not a welfare state, even though Tudor paternalism was evident in the poor law system and More's *Utopia.* All of the elements are there: representative government, some responsibility, however slight, to Parliament, centralization and proclivity to absolutism, and benign welfare legislation. Even in 1559, when the religious question was so prominent, the government of England was more secular than ecclesiastical, although churchmen continued to occupy themselves with statecraft. Elizabeth was concerned equally with the stability of the church and with the stability of the state, believing that the one would contribute to the other.

Awaiting the Religious Settlement, a religious leader wrote about Elizabeth: "She is, however, prudently, and firmly, and piously following up her purpose, though somewhat more slowly than we would wish." [45] Almost all Englishmen welcomed her to the throne of England, fervent in their cry "God save the Queen!"

[45] John Jewel to Henry Bullinger, London, 20 March 1559, *Zurich Letters* (1558—79), I, 10.

CHAPTER II

THE ELIZABETHAN PARLIAMENT OF 1559
ESTABLISHES THE SUPREMACY

onvened on 23 Jan. 1559, Parliament began its actual sessions on the 25th of January and was dissolved on the 8th of May.[1] The main business of the sessions was the Religious Settlement. Sir Anthony Cooke defined the issues: "We are now busy in parliament about expelling the tyranny of the pope, and restoring the royal authority, and re-establishing the true religion. But we are moving far too slowly; nor are there wanting at this time Sanballats and Tobiases [a reference to the bishops] to hinder and obstruct the building of our walls. . . . The zeal of the queen is very great, the activity of the nobility and people is also great; but still the work is hitherto too much at a stand. . . . But the result of this meeting of parliament will, as far as I can judge, confirm my hope.[2]

His hope was the hope of many Englishmen when Elizabeth came to the throne. Few perhaps were willing to see as radical

[1] *Journals of the House of Lords, Beginning Anno Primo Henrici Octavi* (no place of publication, publisher, or date of publication given), I, 542. Hereafter cited as *L. J.*, I. See also *C. J.*, I, 53; Simmonds D'Ewes, *The Journals of All the Parliaments During the Reign of Queen Elizabeth, Both of the House of Lords and House of Commons,* revised by Paul Bowes (London, 1682), pp. 37, 39. Cited as D'Ewes, *Journals.*

[2] Sir Anthony Cooke to Peter Martyr, London, 12 February 1559, *Zurich Letters,* I, 13, 14.

23

a reformation as Cooke wanted, but even among the radicals there was a willingness to settle for less than extreme measures. Elizabeth would not have agreed to extremes. The issue had to be decided by acts of Parliament or the Crown in Parliament. The desire for the reintroduction of Protestantism was due only in part to a reaction to the religious persecutions under Mary. In part it was due to the Spaniards. The progress of Protestantism during the reign of Edward had been such that there were 300 martyrs and 800 exiles during Mary's reign. Nationalism, antisacerdotalism, Lollardy, Lutheranism, Zwinglianism, Calvinism, Anabaptism, humanism, or Erasmianism influenced the English mind. All of these forces played into the Elizabethan Religious Settlement.

Henry VIII had used "the Reformation Parliament" to pass a series of laws to make the English Church independent of Rome. Of these the Act of Supremacy (1534) was by far the most important. The act was brief; in involved legal language it declared the king and his successors to be "the only supreme head in earth of the Church of England, called Anglicana Ecclesia." [3] Other acts had provided, for instance, that the clergy could not enact any ordinances or canons without "the king's most royal assent and licence," that no annates or Peter's pence be paid to Rome, that the succession to the throne be established. [4] The dissolution of the monasteries had followed, also by acts of Parliament at the behest of Henry. [5]

In Edward's reign the first enactment was an "Act against Revilers, and for Receiving in Both Kinds." [6] One Act of Uniformity was passed in 1549; a second, in 1552. [7] They provided for the use of the Book of Common Prayer in the churches.

[3] 26 Henry VIII, cap. 1, Gee and Hardy, *Documents,* No. LV, pp. 243, 244.

[4] 25 Henry VIII, cap. 20—22, ibid., No. LI—LIV, pp. 201—243.

[5] 27 Henry VIII, cap. 28, ibid., No. LXI, 257—268; 31 Henry VIII, cap. 13, ibid., No. LXIV, pp. 281—303.

[6] 1 Edward VI, cap. 1, ibid., No. LXVII, pp. 322—328.

[7] 2 and 3 Edward VI, cap. 1, ibid., No. LXIX, 358—366; 5 and 6 Edward VI, cap. 1, ibid., No. LXXI, pp. 369—372.

Queen Mary's first proclamation about religion stated that she preferred the Old Religion.[8] She used Parliament to repeal the acts of religion, nine in all, passed during the reign of Edward, restoring the *status quo* of 1547.[9] A second act of repeal restored the *status quo of* 1529, setting aside eighteen acts of Henry VIII relating to the church, and one of Edward VI.[10] The heresy acts were revived.

Precedent and right demanded that the Elizabethan Religious Settlement be made by Parliament. Was Parliament simply subservient to the monarch, a sixteenth-century rubber stamp for royal absolutism? The sweep of events might suggest that. The personal monarchy of the Tudors directed the course of legislation. The right of absolute veto belonged to them.[11] To suppose, however, that their legislative bodies followed only the thinking of the monarch, that they had no concept of legislative rights and privileges, or that conferences and petitions were unknown to them, borders almost on the naive. Was Elizabeth's first Parliament "packed"? Were efforts made to get representatives for the House of Commons who would be favorable to the queen and the religious settlement? So, for instance, a Roman Catholic historian suggests that it was packed, at least in part, as was usual, he says, with sixteenth-century parliaments.[12] The foremost English authority on the Elizabethan parliaments denies this:

> The elections to Elizabeth's first Parliament were conducted without recourse to circular letters, such as Mary Tudor had employed in a vain effort to keep Protestants out of her House of Commons: at least, no such letters are known, and the balance of probability is strongly against them. . . . If county elections tended to reflect

[8] Ibid., No. LXXII, pp. 373—376.

[9] 1 Mary, Statute 2, cap. 2, ibid., No. LXXIII, pp. 377—380.

[10] 1 and 2 Philip and Mary, cap. 8, ibid., No. LXXVI, pp. 385—416.

[11] 1 and 2 Philip and Mary, cap. 6, ibid., No. LXXV, p. 384.

[12] Hughes, *Reformation in England,* III, 17 f.

Theodore Maynard, *Queen Elizabeth* (Milwaukee: Bruce Publishing Co., 1940), pp. 77—79.

the character of the government in power, there is nothing mysterious or sinister in that.[13]

The writs summoning this first Parliament had been issued on 5 Dec. 1558 at Westminster.[14] On the 25th of January, after a procession and a solemn service in Westminster Abbey, Sir Nicholas Bacon opened Parliament with an oration. He asked that the laws to be enacted should unite the people of the realm into a uniform order of religion, "to the honour and glory of God, the establishment of His Church, and tranquility of the realm." The chief purpose of this meeting of Parliament, he set forth, was the advancement of God's honour and glory by a settlement of the religious question. The members of Parliament would, in their deliberations, forbear resorting to "all manner of contention, reasoning, disputes, and sophistical, captious, and frivolous arguments and quiddities." He asked them not to use party labels that would increase strife, such as "heretic" or "papist." Nursing factions and sects, or whatever else was an enemy of concord and unity, was to be avoided. Four extremities, as Bacon referred to them, were subject to divine punishment and were to be shunned: "idolatry, superstition, contempt, and irreligion." Moderation was the keynote of the address.[15] The voice was the voice of Bacon, but the hand was the hand of Elizabeth.

The "secular side of the Elizabethan establishment," as it has

[13] Neale, E. & Parl., I, 38, 39. Prothero in the introduction to his Select Statutes, p. xx, says: "The Parliaments of Elizabeth were neither packed nor servile."

J. B. Black, The Reign of Elizabeth, 1558—1603 (Vol. VIII of the Oxford History of England, ed. G. N. Clark; Oxford: The Clarendon Press, 1936 [reprint of 1952]), p. 10: "There was no abnormal packing."

So, too, Pollard, Political History (1547—1603), pp. 199 f.

[14] D'Ewes, Journals, pp. 2, 3, and 37, 38 for samples of these writs.

[15] John Strype, Annals of the Reformation and Establishment of Religion and other various occurrences in the Church of England during Queen Elizabeth's Happy Reign (new edition; Oxford: At the Clarendon Press, 1824), I, i, 78—80. Cited as Strype, Elizabeth.

D'Ewes, Journals, pp. 11, 12. Il Schifanoya to Ottaviano Vivaldino, London, 30 Jan. 1550, Ven. Cal., VII (1558—80), No. 15, pp. 22—24, for a colorful description of the opening of Parliament.

been called,[16] rested on an "Act of Recognition of the Queen's Title," "The Treason Act," and several minor acts. The first of these, "An Act for the Recognition of the Queen's Highness's Title to the Imperial Crown of this Realm," was introduced into the House of Lords early in the session. The act stated that Elizabeth was "in very deed and of most right ought to be, by the laws of God and the laws and statutes of this realm, our most rightful and lawful Sovereign Liege Lady and Queen." The act guaranteed her title to the throne without allowing further questions. Nor should questions be raised about her birth. Was she a legitimate or an illegitimate daughter of Henry VIII and Anne Boleyn? The statute, at least, declared her legitimate without fanfare and elaborate argumentation: ". . . and that your Highness is rightfully, lineally and lawfully descended and come of blood royal of this realm of England, . . ." Her heirs, too, would have the right of succession.[17] Those who maintain that Elizabeth did not concern herself about the legitimacy of her birth have missed one point of this act. More important, however, was the fact that this act was the foundation on which the Act of Supremacy rested. Another act was passed, that "for the restoring of her Blood to her Mother," which simply means that she was restored as her mother's legal heir, or "by which she was qualified, as a private Subject, to succeed, either to her Grandfather's Estate, or to any others by that Blood." [18]

The Treason Act caused more debate in Parliament than the act acknowledging the legitimacy of Elizabeth's claims to the throne. The act provided that anyone who plotted against the Queen's majesty or waged war or rebellion against her should incur

[16] Neale, *E. & Parl.*, I, 45.

[17] 1 Elizabeth, cap. 3, George B. Adams and H. Morse Stephens, eds., *Select Documents of English Constitutional History* (New York: The Macmillan Co., 1910), No. 169, pp. 306, 307; Prothero, *Select Statutes*, p. 21. *L. J.*, I, 545, 546; *C. J.*, I, 54, 56; D'Ewes, *Journals*, pp. 18, 19, 47, 49.

[18] Gilbert Burnet, *The History of the Reformation of the Church of England*, 3d ed. (Dublin: A. Rhames, 1730), part II, book III, Vol. II, 287.
D'Ewes, *Journals*, pp. 19, 20, 21, 47, 48; *L. J.*, I, 54, 55. In each house the bill was given speedy action without any delaying amendments.

the punishments reserved for traitors. Those who would transfer her title to someone else would be liable to the penalties of high treason. Every ecclesiastical person, it was stated explicity, who was convicted of an offense under this act was to be "deprived from all his benefices and promotions spiritual or ecclesiastical." Impeachment for offenses "committed only by open preaching or words" would have to be made within six months of the offense.[19]

Even before these bills were under way in the House of Lords and before bills had been introduced for the alteration of religion, the temper of the House of Commons showed itself in a demand to consider the absence of *Supremum Caput,* the title "Supreme Head of the Church," in the writs of summons to Parliament. The treasurer and twenty-three other members of the House of Commons were to investigate. It was an unusually large committee and certainly too large a committee for its purpose. What intervened between the 30th of January, when the committee was appointed, and the 3d of February, when it reported back, we do not know. To Venice went the report: "Here Parliament goes on briskly, and in the Lower House there was great talk about giving the title of Supreme Head of the Anglican Church *(supremum caput Ecclesiae Anglicanae)* to the Queen, much being said against the Church [of Rome]."[20] Perhaps the Protestants were using this committee as a sounding board, making far-reaching demands for religious changes. At any rate on the 3d of February the committee reported back that the omission of the title did not hinder anything or affect the validity of the present Parliament.[21]

The first bill introduced into the House of Lords bore the title "Act for the Restitution of the First Fruits and Tenths." It was not primarily a revenue act (although the revenue deriving from it would be welcome to the Crown) but a harbinger of the change

[19] 1 Elizabeth, cap. 5, Adams and Stephens, *Select Documents,* No. 170, pp. 307—309; Prothero, *Select Statutes,* pp. 23—25.
L. J., I, 547, 548, 549, 557, 562, 566; *C. J.,* II, 54, 55; D'Ewes, *Journals,* pp. 21, 23, 25, 47, 48, 49.

[20] Il Schifanoya to Ottaviano Vivaldino, London, 6 February 1559, *Ven. Cal.,* VII (1558—80), No. 18, p. 26.

[21] *C. J.,* I, 53, 54; D'Ewes, *Journals,* p. 38; Neale, *E. & Parl.,* I, 46, 47.

of religion. Henry had had such a law, but it had been repealed by Mary's Parliament.[22] In the House of Lords, after the third reading on the 4th of February, the nine spiritual Lords present voted against the passage of the act.[23] This was their first overt act of dissent in the Parliament itself, "by which it may be seen, how unwillingly these Popish Bishops did suffer their Dagon to fall down."[24] The queen's attorney and the solicitor brought the bill to the House of Commons. Here new provisos were added to the Lords' bill.[25] In the House of Lords the spiritual Lords present again voted against the bill when it came up for passage on the 15th of March with amendments.[26] The new provision from the Lords was sanctioned by the House of Commons on the 22d of March.[27] The full title of the act tells its intent: "An Act for the Restitution of the First Fruits and Tenths, and Rents reserved *Nomine Decimae,* and of Parsonages Impropriated to the Imperial Crown of the Realm." The language of the act, which granted certain exemptions to the universities, the colleges, and the schools, was very solicitous for the queen.[28]

Only two acts of the Elizabethan Parliament of 1559, however, belong to the very essence of the Religious Settlement. They are numbered 1 Elizabeth, cap. 1, and 1 Elizabeth, cap. 2, although both of them were actually passed late in this session of Parliament. They are Elizabeth's Supremacy Act and the Act of Uniformity.

"The Elizabethan religious settlement is shrouded in mystery," as Neale remarked.

---

[22] 25 Henry VIII, cap. 20, Gee and Hardy, *Documents,* No. LII, pp. 201 to 209; 1 & 2 Philip and Mary, cap. 8, ibid., No. LXXVI, pp. 385—415.

[23] *L. J.,* I, 544, 545, 546; D'Ewes, *Journals,* pp. 17, 18.

[24] Ibid., p. 19.

[25] *C. J.,* I, 54, 55; D'Ewes, *Journals,* pp. 45 f; 48.

[26] *L. J.,* I, 552, 563; D'Ewes, *Journals,* pp. 21, 23. On the previous day Il Schifanoya wrote Ottaviano Vivaldino, London, 14 March 1559, that this bill was passed. *Ven. Cal.,* VII (1558—80), No. 40, p. 46.

[27] *C. J.,* I, 58; D'Ewes, *Journals,* pp. 51, 52; *L. J.,* I, 568; D'Ewes, *Journals,* p. 25.

[28] 1 Elizabeth, cap. 4; Prothero, *Select Statutes,* pp. 22, 23.

It is a tribute to the enduring qualities of the settlement that in looking back it has seemed natural and inevitable: as though from the beginning there could have been no other policy than that of the middle-way — the *via media* of tradition. But when and how this policy was shaped, or even what happened in Parliament, has been a matter of guesswork, based on the most meagre and baffling evidence. Meagre and baffling the evidence remains. Its scrutiny therefore has to be close — on occasion perhaps even forbiddingly close — if we are to force it, as we can, to yield its dramatic secret.[29]

Neale has examined the evidence carefully.[30] A retracing of his steps belongs to the close scrutiny of the evidence.

On the 9th of February "The Bill to restore the Supremacy of the Church of England, &c. to the Crown of the Realm" was introduced into the House of Commons, given its first reading, and referred to Sir Anthony Cooke,[31] and "as it is very probable, also to some others not named."[32] Cooke may rightly be regarded as an important member of the "Puritan faction,"[33] a not too highly organized number of members who favored the Genevan way. On the 13th of February the bill was given its second reading, designated this time by the clerk as "The Bill annexing the Supremacy to the Crown."[34] On this Monday, all day on Tuesday, the 14th, and again on Wednesday, the measure was debated.[35]

[29] Neale, *E. & Parl.*, I, 51. Cf. p. 60.

[30] J. E. Neale, "The Elizabethan Acts of Supremacy and Uniformity," *English Historical Review*, LXV (July 1950), 304—332. Cited as Neale in *E. H. R.*, LXV (July 1950); Neale, *E. & Parl.*, I, 51—84.

[31] *C. J.*, I, 54.

[32] D'Ewes, *Journals*, p. 45.

[33] Neale, *E. & Parl.*, I, 57. On p. 59 about the selection of Cooke: "That the House chose for this task their most eminent independent *emigre*-Member is surely eloquent testimony to its mood." See also G .W. Dugmore, *The Mass and the English Reformers* (London: Macmillan & Co., Ltd., 1958), ch. IX.

[34] *C. J.*, I, 54.

[35] Ibid. Under 13 February 1559 the entry reads: "Arguments upon the Bill of Supremacy." These same words are entered under 14 February, the only entry for that day.

We do not know by whom the arguments were made or what the arguments were. The final act had twenty-four articles. Probably this first bill, submitted by the government, was a long one. Some conjectures may be permitted. Surely it provided for the repeal of some of the previous legislation, particularly that made on religious questions under Queen Mary. Very likely it also provided for the re-enactment of legislation made during the reign of Edward VI or Henry VIII or both. There may have been considerable debate on a section which proposed the adoption of a heresy act. Those leaning toward the more extreme Protestant views did not want to see persecutions and burnings again. Some of them had just lately returned from exile. The form of the oath and the exact title to be given Elizabeth were debated. Likely — very likely — there was debate about the section which dealt with the Sacrament of the Altar. In the final act it read:

> And that it may please your Highness that it may be enacted by the authority aforesaid, That one Act and Statute made in the first year of the reign of the late King Edward the Sixth, your Majesty's most dear brother, intitled an Act against such persons as shall unreverently speak against the Sacrament of the Body and Blood of Christ, commonly called the Sacrament of the Altar, and for the receiving thereof under both kinds, and all and every branches, clauses and sentences therein contained, shall and may likewise from the last day of this session of Parliament be revived and from thenceforth shall and may stand, remain and be in full force, strength and effect to all intents, constructions and purposes, in such like manner and form as the same was at any time in the first year of the reign of the said late King Edward the Sixth; any law, statute or other matter to the contrary in any wise notwithstanding.[36]

From London it was reported to Venice, 20 February 1559: "As the 'Bill' [to give ecclesiastical authority to the Queen] contains very many clauses, an order became necessary for its examination clause by clause, as they are now doing." *Ven. Cal.,* VII (1558—80), No. 27, p. 35.

[36] 1 Elizabeth, cap. 1, v. Prothero, *Select Statutes,* p. 4; Gee and Hardy, *Documents,* p. 446.

These vestigial remains, "imbedded like a fossil" (to borrow Neale's phrase), seem to be proof enough that no Act of Uniformity was intended by the government and that the worship of the Church of England would be ordered perhaps according to the Sarum liturgy, with Holy Communion celebrated *sub utraque,* bypassing the First and Second Prayer Books of Edward VI. Such, at least, would be the *interim* arrangement. In due time a convocation could fashion a Book of Common Prayer. If this conjecture, made by Neale,[37] is correct, then the debate on the 13th and 14th of February dealt with questions of worship as well as of order. When the great debate ended — for it must be regarded as the most extensive debate of the session, meager as the records are — "Committees were appointed, for the drawing of a new Bill, for annexing of the Supremacy to the Crown."[38] Sir Francis Knollys and Sir Anthony Cooke, both staunch Protestants, are listed[39] as the chairmen, it seems, of the two committees. Again, it is not possible to say what the specific tasks of the committees were or even if there were two committees. The possibility remains that there was only one committee and that there were only two members of this committee.

On the 21st of February the new "Bill for the Supremacy of the Church &c. annexed to the Crown" was given its first reading in the House of Commons. On the following day it was engrossed after the second reading. On the 25th it was read the third time and passed. Neale believes that this bill "revived the 1552 Prayer Book and re-established the religious structure as it was at the death of Edward VI."[40]

This bill, "An Act restoring the Supremacy to the Imperial Crown of this Realm, and repealing divers Acts of Parliament made to the contrary," as it is now called, was sent up to the House of Lords on the 27th day of February. Here it was given its first reading on the 28th. An observer reported that at the

---

37 Neale, *E. & Parl.,* I, 52—54. See also Pollard, *Political History (1547—1603),* p. 201.

38 D'Ewes, *Journals,* p. 47.

39 *C. J.,* I, 54.

40 Neale, *E. & Parl.,* I, 61.

end of February the Commons "decided that the supreme ecclesiastical power was attached to the crown of England."[41] Almost two weeks later, on the 13th of March, it was given its second reading. What caused the delay? Consultations were being held between the queen and members of her government. "It looks very much," Neale remarked, "as if a tussle were going on at Court between radical, moderate, and conservative opinion."[42] At any rate on the 13th of March the bill was committed to a committee of two bishops and thirteen Lords.[43]

Now the Lords amended and altered the Supremacy Bill. The amendments and provisos were given their first reading on the 15th of March, the second on the 17th, and the third reading, together with the bill, on the 18th. An interested outsider reported:

Although the Lower House passed the Bill *(l'articolo)* appointing Queen Elizabeth Supreme Head of the Church, nevertheless in the Upper House, after very great altercations and disputes on the part of the bishops and of other good and pious peers, the question has been consigned to silence for the last few days, and they have discussed certain other matters relating to the kingdom. But in the meanwhile the Court preachers in the presence of her Majesty and the people are doing their utmost to convert the latter, seeking to prove by their false arguments that the Pope has no authority, and uttering the most base and abominable things that were ever heard against the Apostolic See. For this and other reasons many persons are of opinion that the Bill will pass the Upper House likewise, against the consent of the prelates and of other pious lay peers.[44]

[41] London, 29 Feb. 1559 *{sic}*, Martin A. S. Hume, ed. *Calendar of Letters and State Papers Relating to English Affairs, Preserved Principally in the Archives of Simancos* (London: Printed for her Majesty's Stationery office, 1892), Vol. I, Elizabeth, 1558—67, No. 16, p. 33. Cited as *Span. Cal., Eliz.,* I (1558—67).

[42] Neale, *E. & Parl.,* I, 64.

[43] *L. J.,* I, 563; D'Ewes, *Journals,* p. 21.

[44] Il Schifanoya to Ottaviano Vivaldino, London, 14 March 1559, *Ven. Cal.,* VII (1558—80), No. 40, p. 46.

Count Salopp and Viscount Montague together with the ten spirituals present voted against the bill.[45] To this D'Ewes remarked at some length:

Here also we may still note the great lenity and mercy of this great queen, who suffered so many heretical, and obstinately popish Bishops to hold their sees, to have free voices in Parliament, besides the Abbot of Westm', who all thus opposed the just power and authority, which the princes of this realm have, under God himself, under their dominion; and which our ancient kings, under the darkest time of popery, did easily discern, and not improbably did aim at, as we see frequently specified in the ancient and most authentic records of this kingdom. . . .[46]

This version of the bill very likely designated the queen as "Supreme Head of the Church of England, immediate and next unto God." It also eliminated some of the most far-reaching proposals of the House of Commons. A Venetian observer reported:

The Earl of Pembroke, the Earl of Shrewsbury [Talbot], Viscount Montague, and Lord Hastings did not fail in their duty like true soldiers of Christ to resist the Commons, whom they compelled to modify a book passed by the Commons forbidding the Mass to be said or the Communion to be administered *(ne se communicassero)* except at the table in the manner of Edward VI; nor were the Divine offices to be performed in Church; priests likewise being allowed to marry, and the Christian religion and the sacraments being absolutely abolished; adding thereto many extraordinary penalties against delinquents. By a majority of votes they have decided that the aforesaid things shall be expunged from the book, and that the masses, sacraments, and the rest of the Divine office shall be performed as hitherto; but some persons say that this decision cannot last long, the Catholics insisting at any rate on retaining the mass, the offices, and the rest of the sacraments, and the Protestants *(gli Protestanti)* insisting on the contrary. . . . The members of the Lower House, seeing that the Lords passed this article of the Queen's Supremacy of the Church,

45 *L. J.,* I, 564.
46 D'Ewes, *Journals,* pp. 23, 24.

34

but not as the Commons drew it up, — the Lords councelling the aforesaid clauses and modifying some others, — grew angry, and would consent to nothing, but are in very great controversy, as they must of necessity ratify what the Lords have done in the Upper House.[47]

Since changes had been made, it was necessary to refer the bill back to the Commons, where, as noted, the members were angry. This was done on the 18th of March. It was given a first reading in its amended form on the 20th and the next two readings on the two following days.[48] The approval of the Lords' amended bill on the 22d of March, one would suppose, meant that the bill was ready for royal assent.[49] It gave Elizabeth the definite title of "Supreme Head of the Church." [50] This, however, was not the final version of the act.

On this same day, 22 March 1559, the queen issued a proclamation which put into force the provisions noted above regarding Holy Communion. Those making their Easter Communion — the proclamation was issued on Holy Wednesday — would do so under both kinds, receiving both the bread and the wine, in a ceremony or rite spoken in English.[51] The proclamation, it may be noted incidentally, avoided the doctrinal question of the Real Presence or of Transubstantiation.

[47] Il Schifanoya to Ottaviano Vivaldino, London, 21 March 1559, *Ven. Cal.,* VII (1558—80), No. 45, p. 52.
Count de Feria to Philip II, London, 19 March 1559, *Span. Cal., Eliz.,* I (1558—67), No. 18, p. 37, reported that Elizabeth would not take the title "head of the church" but was "resolved to restore religion as her father left it."

[48] *C. J.,* I, 58; D'Ewes, *Journals,* p. 52.

[49] *L. J.,* I, 568; D'Ewes, *Journals,* pp. 25, 26. The House of Commons had added one proviso, evidently of little consequence. This was given three quick readings in the House of Lords and passed with the dissenting vote of ten spiritual Lords.

[50] Il Schifanoya to Ottaviano Vivaldino, London, 11 April 1559, *Ven. Cal.,* VII (1558—80), No. 58, p. 66: "The title of 'Supreme Head of the Church' passed through the two Houses, but her Majesty is expected for some reason not to accept it."

[51] Neale, *E. & Parl.,* I, 67. Il Schifanoya to Ottaviano Vivaldino, London, 28 March 1559, *Ven. Cal.,* VII (1558—80), No. 51, p. 57.

The proclamation spoke of the "present last session of Parliament." Parliament was scheduled to end before Easter. Instead, Parliament was adjourned until the 3d of April. Neale regards this action as "one of the significant moments in English history." He believes that it "altered the pattern of the Elizabethan religious settlement." [52] Had Parliament been adjourned at this time there would have been no Act of Uniformity. Neale's interpretation argues for a shift in the pattern of the Elizabethan Settlement. The united opposition of the Roman Catholic bishops in the House of Lords, the concerted demands of the Puritan faction in the House of Commons and among the royal advisers, and the signing of the peace treaty of Cateau-Cambresis brought about this change.[53] The opposition encountered in the House of Commons most certainly was one important factor in the change of plans. "They are therefore in greater discord than ever," it was reported.[54] And Elizabeth wanted unity. The peace with France was another factor. "I am sure," Count de Feria wrote Philip II, "that the news of peace made the Parliament come to the decision I have mentioned." [55]

This meant another version of the Act of Supremacy, the third version. D'Ewes conjectured that the House did not like the pre-

[52] Neale, E. & Parl., I, 69. However, the decision to adjourn Parliament, not to dissolve it, seems to have come before the night of 23d to 24th of March. Neale has fixed this date. Neale in E. H. R., LXV (July 1950), 324; E. & Parl., I, 69. That this decision may be dated earlier can be seen from a letter by Il Schifanoya to Ottaviano Vivaldino, London, 21 March 1559, Ven. Cal., VII (1558—80), No. 45, p. 52: "Parliament which ought to have ended last Saturday, was prolonged till next Wednesday in Passion Week, and according to report they will return a week after Easter. . . ."

[53] The interpretation is Neale's, vide, E. & Parl., I, 69—71; E.H.R., LXV (July 1950), 324—326. The news of the signing was received on the 19th. Span. Cal., Eliz., I (1558—67), No. 18, p. 38. Cf. No. 21, p. 43.

Pollard, Political History (1547—1603), pp. 203 f. He blamed the temper of the Lower House, developments in foreign affairs, doubts about the validity of the acts, and the warning of Lever for the change.

[54] Il Schifanoya to Ottaviano Vivaldino, London, 28 March 1559, Ven. Cal., I (1558—80), No. 51, p. 57.

[55] London, 24 March 1559, Span. Cal., Eliz. I (1558—67), No. 21, p. 43.

36

vious act or that it had some defect. The Houses had labored long with the former bill, "although it seemeth it came to nothing." [56] The third version was given its first reading in the House of Commons on the 10th of April; the second, on the 12th, when it was engrossed; the third, on the 13th, when it passed. On the 14th it was sent up to the House of Lords, given its first reading on the following day, and on the 17th a second reading. ". . . Parliament has come to no further conclusion," it was reported, "about the title *Supremum Caput in Terris Ecclesiae Anglicanae,*' because her Majesty does not wish it; but they have settled for her to be Governess-General of spiritual and temporal matters in this kingdom. . . ." [57] On the 17th the bill was committed, and one new proviso was added. This proviso was given its first and second readings on the 25th of April, and the third on the 26th. The entire bill was returned to the Lords on the 28th with the new proviso. This, it seems, received the customary three readings in the House of Lords. The bill was passed on the 28th of April. Again the ten spiritual Lords present and Viscount Montague dissented. It was designated as "The Bill to avoid all foreign power used by any foreign potentate in this realm, and for the oath to be taken" and "the bill for restoring the spiritual jurisdiction to the imperial crown of the realm, and abolishing foreign power," or simply "the Bill of Supremacy." [58] It was given royal assent on the 8th of May.[59]

This bill no longer designated Elizabeth as the Supreme Head of the Church. She is called "the only supreme governor." The

[56] D'Ewes, *Journals,* p. 28.

[57] Il Schifanoya to Ottaviano Vivaldino, London, 25 April 1559, *Ven. Cal.,* VII (1558—80), No. 64, p. 73.

Count de Feria to Philip II, London, 18 April 1559, *Span. Cal., Eliz.,* I (1558—67), No. 27, p. 55: "Since then the news is that the Queen having sent to Parliament to say that she did not wish to take the title of 'Head of the Church,' and asking them to think of some other style, they have agreed that she shall be called 'Governess of the Church,' as it appears to them that it is different if put in this way."

[58] *C. J.,* I, 59; *L. J.,* I, 574; D'Ewes, *Journals,* pp. 27—29, 53, 55.

[59] *L. J.,* I, 579.

act itself is a long one and highly technical in many sections. It recites the changes that had been made by Henry VIII and by Mary's act of repeal. This act of repeal is itself repealed. Eight acts made during the reign of Henry VIII are revived. The more important of these forbade appeals to Rome,[60] the sending of annates and first fruits to Rome,[61] and the submission of the clergy.[62] Other acts legislated about marriage.[63] The revival of the Edwardian statute dealing with the Lord's Supper [64] and the repeal of Queen Mary's act reviving the heresy acts [65] were declared explicitly and in detailed fashion "to the intent that all usurped and foreign power and authority, spiritual and temporal, may for ever be clearly extinguished." The law forbade any "foreign prince, person, prelate, state, or potentate, spiritual or temporal" to exercise any power or jurisdiction or authority in the realm. Ecclesiastical authority was annexed to the Crown. Reformation and the correction of heresies were among the powers granted the sovereign. The monarch was given full power to appoint a commission or commissions to carry out the duties and prerogatives of the act.

The act also provided that an oath be administered to "all and every archbishop, bishop, and all and every other ecclesiastical person, and other ecclesiastical officer and minister, of what ever estate, dignity, pre-eminence, or degree soever he or they be or shall be, and all and every temporal judge, justice, mayor, and other lay or temporal officer and minister, and every other person having your highness's fee or wages, within this realm. . . ." The oath read:

[60] 24 Henry VIII, cap. 12, Gee and Hardy, *Documents,* No. L, pp. 187 to 195.

[61] 23 Henry VIII, cap. 20, ibid., No. XLIX, pp. 178—186; 25 Henry VIII, cap. 20, ibid., No. LII, pp. 201—209.

[62] 25 Henry VIII, cap. 19, ibid., No. LI, pp. 195—200.

[63] Parts of the acts 32 Henry VIII, cap. 38, not repealed by 2 & 3 Edward VI, cap. 23, and the act 37 Henry VIII, cap. 17.

[64] 1 Edward VI, cap. 1, ibid., No. LXVII, pp. 322—328.

[65] 1 & 2 Philip and Mary, cap. 6, ibid., No. LXXV, p. 384.

I, A. B., do utterly testify and declare in my conscience, that the queen's highness is the only supreme governor of this realm, and of all other her highness's dominions and countries, as well in all spiritual or ecclesiastical things or causes, as temporal, and that no foreign prince, person, prelate, state or potentate, has, or ought to have, any jurisdiction, power, superiority, pre-eminence, or authority ecclesiastical or spiritual, within this realm; and therefore I do utterly renounce and forsake all foreign jurisdiction, powers, superiorities, and authorities, and do promise that from henceforth I shall bear faith and true allegiance to the queen's highness, her heirs and lawful successors, and to my power shall assist and defend all jurisdictions, pre-eminences, privileges, and authorities granted or belonging to the queen's highness, her heirs and successors, or united and annexed to the imperial crown of this realm. So help me God, and by the contents of this book.

The officers of the realm, ecclesiastical or temporal, who would refuse to take this oath were to be deprived of office. Such refusal, too, would disable them from holding other offices within the realm. Those about to enter office were required to take this oath. Persons suing livery of lands, doing homage, or entering the queen's service were likewise required to take this oath. So, too, were those entering holy orders or accepting a university degree. Those maintaining "by writing, printing, teaching, preaching, express words, deed or act" the authority of any foreign power would on conviction for the first offense be liable to the confiscation of all their real and personal property or imprisonment. The penalty for the third offense was the same as that for high treason. Peers were to be tried by their peers. Those aiding offenders were guilty with the offenders. Care was taken — perhaps this was an amendment added by the House of Commons — to spell out that nothing declared by Parliament now in session was to be declared heresy.[66]

So Parliament established the royal supremacy, having previously acknowledged the queen's title to the crown and allowed her the first fruits and annates. Once more England had repudiated the Bishop of Rome.

[66] 1 Elizabeth, cap. 1, ibid., No. LXXIX, pp. 442—458; Prothero, *Select Statutes,* pp. 1—13.

CHAPTER III

THE ELIZABETHAN PARLIAMENT OF 1559

ESTABLISHES POLITY AND ORDER

The House of Commons of the Parliament of 1559 was much more concerned about establishing Protestantism, particularly Protestant polity and order, than the House of Lords was. The chief proponents of the Genevan way were in the Lower House. Not that opposition from staunch Romanists was absent there, but the opposition of the Roman clerics was concentrated in the House of Lords. In the Lower House, too, confirmation of land grants and leases made by bishops of Edward's reign was sought; this involved the whole question of ecclesiastical polity. Not much legislation was passed on this score. Some of the bills which were introduced were measures against the Old Religion; some were trial balloons to test the strength of Protestantism in the House; some were Puritan demands for changes in worship and order. The laconic entries of the clerks of both houses permit room for speculation in accord with other known facts.

Almost at the outset of Parliament the House of Commons gave the first reading to "The Bill for Order of Services and Ministers in the Church." [1] Nothing is known about the author of the bill or its content. Did the bill contain a comprehensive program for the establishment of polity and order in the Church of England,

---

[1] *C. J.*, I, 54; D'Ewes, *Journals*, p. 47. This was on 15 Feb. 1559.

41

perhaps along the lines of the Genevan order of service and ecclesiastical discipline? [2] The very next day another bill was introduced and given its first reading in the House of Commons, "The Book of Common Prayer and Ministration of Sacraments." [3] This bill probably aimed at the restoration of the Second Book of Common Prayer of Edward VI.[4] Credence is given to this view by the fact that a month later, on the 17th of March, the first and second readings were given to "A Bill, that no Persons shall be punished for using the Religion used in King E.'s last year." On the next day it was given a third reading and passed.[5] This bill was read once — only once — in the House of Lords.[6] A trustworthy rumor said that this bill provided for the receiving of the Eucharist at tables.[7] "Everything will be done as in the time of King Edward." [8]

Reports and counterreports about changes in religion were rife. An episode in the House of Commons illustrates the tensions in Parliament. The clerk reported it in these words: "Mr. Chancellor of the Duchy complained, that Sir T. White had called him a witness, not to like the Book of Common Service: — Mr. White answered, that Mr. Chancellor said he wished the Book to be well considered: but for that the House doth take, that Mr. White did

[2] Only the title of the bill is the basis for this conjecture.

[3] *C. J.*, I, 54; D'Ewes, *Journals*, p. 47. This was on 16 Feb. 1559.

[4] Neale, *E. & Parl.*, I, 60, speaks simply of "the restoration of the religious situation at the death of Edward VI." See also Neale in *E. H. R.*, LXV (July, 1950), 313—316. His arguments that this was not the Genevan Prayer Book are convincing, even though he does cite evidence that could be interpreted as pointing to the Genevan book. There is a possibility that this was the revised version of the second Edwardian Book of Common Prayer used in Frankfort. Neale's presentation favors the interpretation that this was the *First* Book of Common Prayer.

[5] *C. J.*, I, 58; D'Ewes, *Journals*, p. 52.

[6] 20 March 1559; *L. J.*, I, 566; D'Ewes, *Journals*, p. 25. Here it is called "An Act to take away all pains and penalties made for religion in Queen Mary's time."

[7] Il Schifanoya to Vivaldino, London, 21 March 1559, *Ven. Cal.*, VII (1558—80), No. 45, p. 52.

[8] The same to the same, London, 25 April 1559, ibid., VII (1558 to 1580), No. 64, p. 73.

mistake him, therefore Mr. White, standing, asked him forgiveness, which Mr. Chancellor did take thankfully."[9] Which "Book of Common Service" is meant? Probably the one last in use, the Second Book of Edward VI.

Hardly had the House of Commons passed the bill which would legalize the use of religion as in the last year of Edward VI and sent it to the Lords when a bill was introduced "to revive the Statutes for Keeping of Holidays."[10] It sought to restore the conditions in early 1553 by the restoration of the church calendar of the Second Prayer Book. No further action was taken until after the Easter recess. Then the bill, referred to more specifically as "The Bill to revive the Act for Holidays and Fasting-Days," was read again.[11] The Commons passed the bill on the 12th of April, naming it still more specifically, "The Bill for Holidays, and Fasting-Days, as in 5° E. VI."[12] It was read twice in the House of Lords.[13] No further mention is made of this bill. Although abortive, it is important. It helps to prove that there was a concerted effort to reintroduce the religious practices of the time of the Second Book of Common Prayer. The observance of Sunday was made mandatory according to this bill. No day, the act declared, was dedicated to a saint, but only to God in remembrance of such saints. Laborers and fishermen might work on saints' days "if need so required, in or out of harvest." On Fridays and Saturdays in Lent abstinence from eating meat was stipulated; the eves of holy days were designated as fast days.[14]

The Puritan faction in Parliament wanted to regulate religious practices outside or beyond the Act of Supremacy. These practices were to agree with those of the last year of Edward's reign. This

[9] C. J., I, 56; D'Ewes, Journals, p. 50.

[10] C. J., I, 58.

[11] C. J., I, 59; D'Ewes, Journals, p. 53. Read and engrossed 4 April 1559

[12] C. J., I, 59.

[13] D'Ewes, Journals, p. 27. On 14 and 15 April 1559.

[14] Burnet, History of the Reformation, 3d ed., part ii, book i, Vol. II, 146.

program is made still clearer by another bill. While the House of Commons was considering the bill to restore the "religion used in K. E.'s last year" and the act for holy days, it also had under consideration a bill "that the Queen's highness shall collate or appoint bishops in bishoprics being vacant and with what rites and ceremonies."[15] The stipulated "rites and ceremonies" was the ordinal of Edward VI. It may have included regulations about vestments. There was very little debate on this measure in the House of Commons.[16] Three readings followed in the House of Lords.[17] The bill was not referred to a committee in either house. However, it did not receive royal assent on the 8th of May.[18] The bill, evidently not a government measure, is of no great importance.

The polity of the Church of England, as a continuation of previous polity, a hierarchical form of church government with archbishops, bishops, priests, and deacons, was sanctioned by the Bill of Supremacy with the revival of the Ecclesiastical Appointments Act of Henry VIII.[19]

The independent effort to prescribe the rites and ceremonies for the consecrating of bishops and archbishops failed. It was promoted during Holy Week, when it seemed that Parliament would be adjourned speedily. Perhaps with the adoption of the Second Book of Common Prayer it was regarded as an unnecessary measure. In the weeks after Easter the measure known as the Act of Uniformity was presented in both Houses and eventually became law.

Still there was a two-week delay after the Easter recess. Very likely the Act of Uniformity was drafted during this period after

[15] *C. J.,* I, 58; D'Ewes, *Journals,* p. 52. D'Ewes, "and without rites and ceremonies," must have made an error in transcription.

[16] *C. J.,* I, 58. It was given the first and second readings on 21 March, passed on the 22d, and sent to the House of Lords on the same day.

[17] *L. J.,* I, 568; D'Ewes, *Journals,* p. 26. On the 22d, too, it was read the first and second time in the House of Lords; it was passed on the 24th after its third reading.

[18] *L. J.,* I, 579, does not list it among the acts receiving royal asssent; nothing is said about a veto.

[19] 1 Elizabeth, cap. 1 received 25 Henry VIII, cap. 20, Gee and Hardy, *Documents,* No. LXXIX, p. 444; Prothero, *Select Statutes,* p. 3.

consultations by the Queen with her councillors, parliamentary leaders of the more extreme Protestant faction, and perhaps Puritan divines.[20] The little or no debate in the House of Commons when the bill was finally presented may be taken as a proof for such consultations; it is not a proof of unanimity of belief on rites and ceremonies. The bill was given three readings in the House of Commons on three successive days, the 18th, 19th, and 20th of April. The clerk designated it as "The Bill for the Unity of the Service of the Church, and Ministration of the Sacraments" on the first day; "The Bill for Uniformity of Common Prayer and Service in the Church," on the second day; "The Bill for Unity of Service in the Church, and Administration of the Sacraments," on the third day. It was engrossed after the second reading, as was customary.[21] There may have been some debate on this day, but there is not even a record that the bill was committed. The failure to refer this bill to a committee seems extremely odd, since the measure was of the greatest importance. The issues had been debated and resolved in other connections, possibly in connection with the debates on the various Bills of Supremacy and other measures not passed, very possibly, too, in conferences outside Parliament.

On the 25th of April the bill was sent up from the House of Commons to the House of Lords. Here it was given its first reading on the 26th and debated, after the second reading, on the 27th. The Romanists had their last formal opportunity in Parliament to protest against the changes in religion. On the 28th the bill was given its third reading. It was passed by a margin of three votes; nine spiritual Lords and nine temporal Lords voted against the bill.[22] The records are very incomplete at this point. A proviso or amendment, added by the House of Lords, and referred to the House of Commons, received speedy approval, and was reported back to the House of Lords on the 29th of April.[23]

[20] Neale, *E. & Parl.*, I, 78, 79.

[21] *C. J.*, I, 60; D'Ewes, *Journals*, p. 54.

[22] D'Ewes, *Journals*, pp. 27, 28, 30.

[23] D'Ewes, too, was puzzled by the lacunae in the records at this point.

This proviso or amendment is found at the end of the act, where it is strangely out of place. It belongs after the exceptions made to the Second Book of Common Prayer and (with a slight modification of language) before the penalty paragraphs. The proviso restrained the more radical demands of the Protestant or Puritan faction in the House of Commons and suited the demands of the more conservative queen.[24] At this time the final effort, outside Parliament, for a radical change in the regulations for the appointments for the churches failed. Seven years later Grindal wrote in connection with the Vestiarian Controversy:

> We who are now bishops, on our first return, and before we entered on our ministry, contended long and earnestly for the removal of those things that have occasioned the present dispute; but as we were unable to prevail, either with the queen or the parliament, we judged it best, after a consultation on the subject, not to desert our churches for the sake of a few ceremonies, and those not unlawful in themselves, especially since the pure doctrine of the gospel remained in all its integrity and freedom; . . . And we do not regret our resolution; for in the meantime, the Lord giving the increase, our churches are enlarged and established, which under other circumstances would have become a prey to the Ecebolians, Lutherans, and semi-papists.[25]

They compromised about ornaments, but they were not ready to substitute the First Prayer Book for the Second.

The ornaments to be used in the church, the bill stated, were to be those of the second year of the reign of Edward VI; the radical changes made in the last two years of his reign were not to be followed, even though the Second Prayer Book was sanctioned. The queen was given authority to make changes "with the advise of her commissioners appointed and authorized . . . or of the metropolitan of this realm." A loophole, too, was permitted the queen if the opposition to the new order became too violent. Con-

---

[24] Neale, *E. & Parl.*, I, 79, does not specify this juncture for the inserting of the Ornaments Rubric.

[25] Edmund Grindal to Henry Bullinger, London, 27 August 1566, *Zurich Letters,* I (1558—79), 169.

tempt and irreverance to the rites and ceremonies or the misuse of orders appointed in the book could be the occasion for revisions, on the advice of the commissioners and archbishop, "as may be most for the advancement of God's glory, the edifying of His Church, and the due reverence of Christ's holy mysteries and sacraments." [26]

But what about the opposition in the House of Lords? The vote of the nine spiritual peers was surely on theological and ecclesiological grounds. Several of the temporal peers, like Montague, voted against the act because of their Roman Catholic predilections. Several of them, to follow Neale's interpretation, "presumably knew and shared the Queen's personal views, felt that she had been coerced and out-manoeuvred by the radicals, and voted as they did in order to strengthen the final, conservative move over the veto." [27] A vote against the bill would not be misunderstood by the queen; it would give an opportunity to a North or a Rich to voice personal convictions. The narrow margin by which the bill was passed ought not to be construed as a proof that the country was not ready for the change in religion.

The remainder of the bill provided for a decided change in religious practices. It repealed Mary's act of repeal, by which the Second Act of Uniformity under Edward VI had been made of no effect.[28] The Second Book of Common Prayer, with a few alterations,[29] was appointed to be used in the churches after the 24th of June. It established the order of services, the rites and ceremonies of the church, and the church calendar.

The penalties provided for offenders against this act were severe. Any parson, vicar, or minister who would refuse to use the prescribed rites or would "willfully and obstinately" use another rite

[26] 1 Elizabeth, cap. 2, Gee and Hardy, *Documents,* No. LXXX, p. 466; Prothero, *Select Statutes,* p. 20.

[27] Neale, *E. & Parl.,* I, 80.

[28] 1 Mary, statute 2, ca. 2, repealed 5 & 6 Edward VI, cap. 1. Gee and Hardy, *Documents,* No. LXXI, pp. 369—372 for the Edwardian statute; ibid., LXXIII, pp. 377—380 for the Marian statute.

[29] *Vide infra,* Ch. IV, for a detailed discussion of the Elizabethan Book of Common Prayer.

or ceremony would upon conviction be deprived of "the profit of all his spiritual benefices or promotions" for a whole year and be imprisoned for six months. A second offense upon conviction would bring a year's imprisonment and deprivation of all spiritual promotions. The third offense, again upon due conviction, would bring on life imprisonment. Life imprisonment was the penalty for the second conviction for anyone who did not have a spiritual promotion. The severity of the penalties extended also to the laity. The laity was enjoined to attend divine services on Sundays and holy days, "there to abide orderly and soberly," unless there was a "lawful or reasonable excuse to be absent." To the censures of the church was added a fine of twelve pence for conviction on noncompliance. The enforcement of this part of the act was given to the bishops, justices of the peace, and other civil officials.

> And for due execution hereof, the queen's most excellent majesty, the Lords temporal (sic), and all the Commons, in this present Parliament assembled, do in God's name earnestly require and charge all the archbishops, bishops, and other ordinaries, that they shall endeavour themselves to the uttermost of their knowledge, that the due execution hereof may be had throughout their dioceses and charges, wherewith Almighty God may justly punish His people for neglecting this good and wholesome law.

Safeguards were written into law, e. g., a time limit was set for prosecuting offenders, and no one was to be punished more than once for the same offense.[30]

The penal provisions of the act made the bishops civil officers. A Roman Catholic historian pointed out: "One novel feature of the penal clauses of this Act of Uniformity is that the bishops are given explicit assurance that they can, with impunity, use all their spiritual powers to correct with excommunication those who offend against it; the spiritual authority of the bishops now derives from that of the queen — there is no longer any reason to fear it for its own sake." [31] The statement is technically accurate, since the

[30] 1 Elizabeth, cap. 2, Gee and Hardy, *Documents,* No. LXXX, pp. 458 to 467; Prothero, *Select Statutes,* pp. 13—20.

[31] Hughes, *Reformation in England,* III, 34.

spiritual power was granted by Parliament, both in this Act of Uniformity and in the revival of the Henrician Ecclesiastical Appointment Act, to the ruler. True, cathedral chapters were permitted to elect bishops on the nomination of the monarch, but they were required to endorse the royal nomination. The election, the confirmation of the election, and the directives for consecration were to come by the decree of the king (or queen). It is "out of the king's hands" that power comes to the bishops; "all possessions and profits spiritual and temporal," the act said, are from that source.[32] In actual practice, to be sure, the episcopal office was not divested of its ecclesiastical significance to the extent that laymen and nonchurchmen were appointed to these positions.

That a proper and acceptable group of men occupy the bishoprics was a concern of members of the House of Commons. We should like to think that these were the same members who were acting with some degree of unanimity in matters of religious reforms. In other words, it appears that the more extreme Protestants wanted to make sure that the bishops would be from among them. For that reason a bill was introduced into the House of Commons on the 15th of March to restore the bishops and other spiritual persons deprived in the time of Queen Mary.[33] The bill was given a second reading on the 6th of April — significantly again after the Easter recess and while the question of the Prayer Book was still being discussed outside Parliament — and referred to a committee.[34] This bill was killed in committee, by government pressure. Another bill, which met with a similar fate, was "The Bill to restore Spiritual Persons, that were deprived for Marriage or Heresies, to be restored to their benefices."[35] The bill, to judge by the title, was too sweeping for proper execution, nor did it meet the favor of those promoting the queen's legislation.

A measure introduced into the House of Commons on the 2d of March came from an extremist of the other side, not from the

[32] 25 Henry VIII, cap. 20, Gee and Hardy, *Documents*, No. LII, pp. 204 to 209

[33] *C. J.*, I, 57; D'Ewes, *Journals*, p. 51.

[34] *C. J.*, I, 59; D'Ewes, *Journals*, p. 53.

[35] *C. J.*, I, 59.

extreme Protestants. It was a discordant note in the voices demanding reform. "The Bill confirming the Bishopric of London to the now Bishop of London," i. e., to Edmund Bonner, must have been introduced by a Romanist, perhaps as a test of strength. The bill received one reading and was heard of no more.[36] A countermeasure to such a bill was proposed by "The Bill to make lawful the Deprivation of the Bishops of London, Wynchester, Wygorn, and Chichester [and Spiritual Persons] in the time of K. E. the VIth." This bill was given only two readings.[37]

At the very end of the session an act that the "Queen by Commission may examine the causes of deprivation of spiritual persons and restore them again" was introduced into the House of Commons, where it received three readings.[38] The Lords also gave it three readings.[39] However, the bill was not given royal assent on the 8th of May.[40] Perhaps it was thought that the Act of Supremacy allowed for such action if desirable; perhaps it was regarded as a restrictive piece of legislation. The progress of the bill points to the strong desire on the part of members of the Parliament to make detailed regulations in Parliament for the ordering of the church and an equally strong desire to go back to the Edwardian Settlement. A final gesture of this kind was a bill engrossed after its first reading, which, however, got no further, "The Bill to make Deprivations of Bishops, and Spiritual Persons, in the Time of K. E. the VIth, pleadable."[41]

Then, too, in the ordering of the polity of the church there were the acts dealing with leases and land grants. Two acts were given assent by the queen on the 8th of May, when her first Parliament was prorogued, assuring lands to certain individuals.

[36] *C. J.*, I, 56; D'Ewes, *Journals*, p. 49.

[37] *C. J.*, I, 58; D'Ewes, *Journals*, pp. 51, 52. On 16 March and 21 March 1559

[38] *C. J.*, I, 61; D'Ewes, *Journals*, p. 55. On 27 April, 29 April, and 2 May 1559

[39] D'Ewes, *Journals*, pp. 30, 31. *L. J.*, I, has no entry about this act. 2 May, 3 May, and 5 May 1559.

[40] Not listed in *L. J.*, I, 579.

[41] *C. J.*, I, 61. On 3 May 1559.

They were "An Act for the Assurance of Lands, late Parcel of the Bishopric of Winchester, to divers Patentees of King Edward the Sixth," and "An Act for the Assurance of certain Lands to the Lord Wentworth, Lord Ryche, and Lord Darcye of Checkie." [42] The first of these bills introduced into the House of Commons was referred to a committee.[43] A new bill was introduced,[44] which was followed by legal hearings. The Bishop of Winchester asked for a copy of the bill and was granted the right to bring in a lawyer to argue the case. The House also granted the patentees the right to be represented by counsel. The bishop contended that these lands had belonged to the diocese of Winchester for 1,300 years. The records were duly examined. In the end the titles to the lands were approved to the queen and the patentees of Edward VI.[45] The House of Lords passed the bill with the dissenting vote of ten spiritual Lords and four temporal Lords.[46]

The second of the acts approved by the queen had fewer difficulties than the former one. The House of Commons approved the bill guaranteeing title to these lands to Wentworth, Rich, and Darcy.[47] The House of Lords passed it with three dissenting votes. Bonner, the bishop of London was, of course, one of the dissenting voters.[48]

"The Bill to confirm Leases and Grants by D. Rydley, Bishop of

[42] *L. J.*, I, 579.

[43] *C. J.*, I, 54, 55; D'Ewes, *Journals*, pp. 47, 48. On 15 Feb. 1559.

[44] *C. J.*, I, 56; D'Ewes, *Journals*, p. 49. Introduced on 28 Feb. 1559.

[45] *C. J.*, I, 56; D'Ewes, *Journals*, p. 50.
The bill was given its second reading on 9 March, likely with some kind of amendments which made two further readings necessary. It is designated in *C. J.*, I, 57, as "L. 2," which means that it was a bill from the House of Lords, being given its second reading. There is no bill of this kind reported from the House of Lords.
The amendments were read on 16 March, when the bill was engrossed, and on 18 March, when it was passed. *C. J.*, I, 58; D'Ewes, *Journals*, p. 51.

[46] *C. J.*, I, 56; D'Ewes, *Journals*, p. 49. Read on 20, 21, and 22 March 1559.

[47] *C. J.*, I, 56; D'Ewes, *Journals*, p. 49. Read on 27 Feb., 1 March, and 3 March 1559.

[48] *L. J.*, I, 557, 559, 560, 561. Read on 7, 8, 9 March 1559.

London, deceased," introduced into the House of Commons, was a very comprehensive measure, which failed of passage but demonstrates, nevertheless, the concern of this House with ordering the temporal affairs of the church. In the words of the clerk, the Bishop of London required a copy of the bill "put in for confirmations of leases granted by Doctor Rydley, Usurper of the Bishoprick, as he saith." He argued that the bill was untrue and "that the commissioners for his deprivation did not according to their commission, and yet by his appeal, as also by his letters patents from Queen Mary, he standeth still Bishop, and the Grants made by N. Rydley void." [49] In spite of the protest the bill was passed by the House of Commons.[50] In the House of Lords the bill "to make good leases, grants of offices, and copyholds, made by Nicholas Ridley, Late Bishop of London," was rejected.[51] It is not evident what the defects in the bill were. Perhaps its chief defect was that it was being promoted by a group of extremists.

There were other efforts by the House of Commons to establish legal title to lands which had passed out of the hands of the church. The Bishop of Worcester and the Bishop of Coventry and Litchfield, too, tried to prevent such actions.[52] A private bill to

[49] C. J., I, 57; D'Ewes, Journals, p. 51. Introduced on 9 March 1559; second reading on 11 March.

[50] C. J., I, 60; D'Ewes, Journals, p. 54. On 15 April 1559.

[51] D'Ewes, Journals, pp. 27, 28. On 30 April 1559 it was given two readings. L. J., I, 577; D'Ewes, Journals, p. 30. It was read the third time on 1 May.

[52] On 4 March the first reading was given in the House of Commons to a bill to assure Hartelbury and Wychenford, which had been under the jurisdiction of the Bishop of Worcester, to Sir Francis Jobson and Walter Blount. C. J., I, 56; D'Ewes, Journals, p. 50. The Bishop of Worcester appeared before the House of Commons with his counsel. He "declared, that Hooper was not lawful Bishop, by reason of the appeal of Bishop Heathe; and so the grant not good; and prayed the House to consider it." D'Ewes, Journals, p. 51. The bill was given its third reading by the House of Commons on 21 March. C. J., I, 58. A new bill was introduced on 15 April, "for assurance of lands, parcel of the Bishoprick of Worcester, to Sir Francis Jobson and Walter Blount," C. J., I, 59; D'Ewes, Journals, p. 54. There seems to have been no further action.

The Bishop of Coventry and Litchfield appeared before the House of Commons on 8 March. C. J., I, 58; D'Ewes, Journals, p. 51.

52

discharge a fine levied by the latter against a certain T. Fisher for rent may have been a demonstration of antiprelacy.[53] A general bill, "The Bill confirming divers Grants and Leases made by Bishops deprived," was introduced into the House of Commons.[54] An effort was also made in the House of Lords to regulate leases made by spiritual persons.[55] Articles were also devised for the punishment of those guilty of canceling land records.[56] All such attempted legislation shows the attitude of the extremists.

One more effort by extremists to control the order and polity of the church must be noted. Already at the end of February "The Bill for Making Ecclesiastical Laws by Thirty-Two Persons" was introduced into the House of Commons.[57] In the House of Lords it received only its first reading.[58] The bill proposed the revival of the commission, already set up by Henry VIII, to revise the laws of the church. The *Reformatio legum ecclesiasticarum,* drafted by this commission, had never been sanctioned by Parliament or even by royal action.[59] It raised two concerns for the Governess-to-be of the church. The one was the question of the responsibility for church laws. Did it belong to the queen or to Parliament? The second looked to the possible radical nature of such a commission and its formulations, perhaps out of all harmony with the queen

[53] Read the second time in the House of Commons on 20 March 1559. *C. J.,* I, 58. Not passed.

[54] *C. J.,* I, 54, 55; D'Ewes, *Journals,* p. 48. Introduced on 11 Feb.; second reading on 18 Feb. 1559.

On 21 February either a new bill on this subject was introduced into the House of Commons or the old bill was given a third reading. *C. J.,* I, 55, listed it as receiving a first reading and does not say that action was taken. No further notice of this bill, however, shows up in the Lower House.

[55] D'Ewes, *Journals,* p. 26. It was referred to a committee of the Lords on 5 April. *L. J.,* I, 570.

[56] *C. J.,* I, 57; D'Ewes, *Journals,* p. 51. On 14 March 1559.

[57] *C. J.,* I, 55, 56, 57; D'Ewes, *Journals,* p. 49. It was given the second reading on 1 March and passed 17 March 1559.

[58] *L. J.,* I, 566, 568; D'Ewes, *Journals,* p. 25. It was sent up on 20 March and given a reading on 22 March 1559.

[59] Neale, *E. & Parl.,* I, 63 f.

53

and her policies. This bill was part "of an organized movement operating through the House of Commons, the object of which was to force upon Elizabeth and her government a complete Protestant programme, at least as radical as that achieved by the close of Edward VI's reign." [60] Of the less than moderate tone of the *Reformatio legum ecclesiasticarum* the articles on heresies and on the Lord's Supper give ample evidence. It provided also for the organizing of church courts and regulated the attendance at church services. [61] The commission was never authorized. However, it is significant that such a commission was desired by the House of Commons, although it failed of authorization by the House of Lords and, of course, the queen.

Two measures which passed and were sanctioned by the queen, disposing of certain church properties, must yet be noted. The one is "An Act, That the Queen's Majesty, upon the Avoidance of any Archbishoprick or Bishoprick, may exchange the Temporal Possessions thereof with Parsonages Impropriate, &c." It was introduced into the House of Lords, undoubtedly as a government measure, immediately after the Easter recess. With the dissenting vote of the spiritual lords it was deferred to the House of Commons. [62] After an unexplainable delay [63] the bill was given a third reading. A division was called for. One hundred thirty-four voted for the bill; ninety voted against it. [64] The bill gave the queen a large amount of leeway for strengthening the finances of the Crown. "A bad bargain it was for the Church," says Neale with justice. [65] What about the votes in the Commons recorded against

[60] Ibid., I, 64.

[61] Hughes, *Reformation in England*, II, 129—134.

[62] *L. J.*, I, 570, 571; D'Ewes, *Journals*, pp. 26, 27. It was introduced on 4 April and given a second reading on 5 April. On 6 April it was referred to a committee and engrossed; on 7 April it was read a third time. D'Ewes pointed out that there is no precedent for this that a bill is held over one day and then committed.

[63] *C. J.*, I, 59; D'Ewes, *Journals*, p. 53. On 7 April it was given its first reading and its second on 8 April.

[64] *C. J.*, I, 60; D'Ewes, *Journals*, p. 54.

[65] Neale, *E. & Parl.*, I, 74.

54

the bill? Neale regards the ninety dissenting voters as those who made up the Puritan faction. He says: "We probably have here an indication of the irreducible Puritan core in this Parliament of 1559: godly men who joyously harried the Papists, but would not betray the Church in the interest of the State." [66] If this interpretation is correct, the vote might have served as a warning to Elizabeth.

The other measure which these Puritans did not oppose, was "The Bill for the Dissolution of Houses of Monasteries, Abbies, Priories, &c. erected since the Death of King Edward the VIth." [67]

With that act the establishing of polity and order, so far as this Parliament was concerned, was accomplished. Compromises were made to bring about this settlement. Problems remained for the church. Elizabeth had leaned more toward a conservative reformation than did some of the Genevans in the House of Commons. She wanted unity within the nation and a strong monarchy. Nicholas Bacon expressed this in his speech when closing Parliament on 8 May 1559 — given here in a seventeenth-century version:

And as to the third, which is the Observation of the uniform Order in Religion; you are to endeavour your selves to the best of your powers and understandings, drawing together in one line all points, to further, set forth and maintain the same, which by great and deliberate advice here in Parliament hath been established. And here great Observations and watch should be had of the withdrawers and hinderers thereof; and especially of those, that subtilly, by indirect means, seek to procure the contrary. Amongst these I mean to comprehend, as well those that be too

[66] Ibid., I, 74 f.

[67] *C. J.*, I, 60, 61; D'Ewes, *Journals,* pp. 31, 55, 56. It was introduced into the House of Commons on 24 April and given its first reading; the second reading followed the next day. It was referred to a committee, although this is not stated; several provisos were added which were read twice on 28 April. On the following day the bill was passed and sent up to the House of Lords. The House of Lords added several other provisos, which in turn were referred to the House of Commons and allowed by it, only two days before the adjournment of this Parliament.

swift, as those that be too slow; those, I say, that go before the Laws, or beyond the Laws, as those that will not follow; for good Government cannot be where obedience faileth, and both these alike break the Rule of Obedience; And these be those, who in likelyhood should be beginners, and maintainers, and upholders, of all Factions and Sects, the very Mother and Nurses to all Seditions and Tumults, which necessarily bring forth destruction and Depopulation; of these therefore great heed would be taken, and upon these being found, sharp and severe Correction (according to the Order of Laws) should be imposed; and that in the beginning, without respect of persons, as upon the greatest adversaries that can be to Unity and Concord, without which no Common-Wealth can long endure and stand; whereupon (you know) all our standing and falling wholly consisteth, and the surety of our Sovereign. Also a matter most marvellous, that Laws whereby men possess all that they have, and their lives also, should not be able to direct men's actions so, as thereby all Factions and Sects, founded for the most part either upon Will, or upon the Glory of men's Wits and Inventions, should not sufficiently be repressed.[68]

[68] D'Ewes, *Journals,* p. 34.

CHAPTER IV

THE PRAYER BOOK OF QUEEN ELIZABETH

S oon after the passage of "An Acte for the Uniformitie of Common Praier, and Seruice in the Church, and the Administration of the Sacraments," *The Boke of Common Praier, and Administration of the Sacraments, and Other Rites and Ceremonies in the Churche of England* was published.[1] Besides the rites and forms to be used in the church, it contained an almanac, a calendar of lessons, a short treatise on ceremonies, and a preface. It was to be used not only by the minister of the church but also by the hearers or worshipers.

The purposes of the Prayer Book are discussed in the preface. By the calendar a scheme was set forth that made possible the reading of the entire Bible during a year. For the clergy the reading of the Scriptures meant that thereby they would be stirred up to godliness. Thereby, too, they would be better able to exhort others through wholesome doctrine and to confute adversaries of the truth. The people would grow in the knowledge of God and in their love of His true religion. Uniform rites and ceremonies would be followed throughout the whole realm. The Prayer Book provided for the use of the English language in the services of the

---

[1] I have used the version in *Liturgies and Occasional Forms of Prayer Set Forth in the Reign of Queen Elizabeth* edited for the Parker Society by William K. Clay (Cambridge: The University Press, 1847), 23—245 (cited hereafter as *Liturgical Services*), and the edition prepared by Edward Benham, *The Prayer-Book of Queen Elizabeth 1559* (Edinburgh: John Grant, 1909).

church. Morning and evening prayers were to be said in the churches and chapels of the realm, and to be omitted only for valid cause. It ordered nothing was to be read, the preface stated, "but the very pure Word of God, the Holy Scriptures, or that which is evidently grounded upon the same, and that in such a language and order, as is most easy and plain for the understanding both of the readers and of the hearers." [2]

The Prayer Book of 1559 was divided into twenty-one sections, as may be seen from the table of contents:

THE CONTENTES OF THIS BOOKE

[2] Ibid., p. 16.

xviii. The Communion of the sicke.

xix. Buriall.

xx. The Thankesgeuing of women after childebyrth.

xxi. A Communacion againste synners, wyth certayne prayers to be vsed diuerse tymes in the yeare.[3]

The Psalter and the Ordinal have been included in the Book of Common Prayer. The Ordinal consists of three services, originally printed as a separate book, "The forme and manner of makynge and consecrating Bishoppes, Priestes, and Deacons."[4]

Thomas Cranmer was the chief author of the first two, and, with that, of the third. Cranmer was an outstanding scholar, a good theologian, a master of English prose. To him the Anglican Prayer Book owes much of its lasting beauty. Cranmer also drew on ancient and current sources for the compilation of his liturgies.

The Litany, published in 1544, followed the invocations, deprecations, pleadings, intercessions, and supplications in the same order as found in the Sarum Litany. For it Cranmer also used other sources. Marshall's *Primer* of 1535 contained a litany which owed much to Martin Luther. Archbishop Hermann von Wied, archbishop of Cologne, had published his *Consultation;* Martin Bucer and Philip Melanchthon had a large hand in this. The Prayer of St. Chrysostom, from the Easter Liturgy of St. Chrysostom, was translated by Cranmer. Of this litany Cranmer wrote to Henry VIII: "I was constrained to use more than the liberty of a translator; for in some processions I have altered divers words; in some I have taken part away; some I have left out whole . . . ; and some processions I have added whole."[5] Cranmer was a compiler and an adapter. The outcome was superb. The Litany remains one of the literary and devotional monuments of the English Reformation.

[3] Ibid., p. 8.

[4] Ibid., p. 157; see pp. 157—181.

[5] Quoted by Francis Procter, *A History of the Book of Common Prayer with a Rationale of Its Offices* (London: Macmillan and Co., 1889), p. 21 n. For a more detailed discussion see my article "Cranmer's Legacy," *Concordia Theological Monthly,* XXVII (April 1956), 241—268.

Cranmer is largely responsible, with a formidable committee of bishops and theologians, for the formation of the Order of Communion in English. It required that proper notice be given of the celebration of the Eucharist, inviting those who wish to participate to come to the parson, vicar, or curate for confession and absolution. The exhortation, general confession, and absolution preceded the distribution of the elements. The distribution was to be accompanied by the words: "The body of our Lord Jesus Christ, which was given for thee, preserve thy body unto everlasting life. . . . The blood of our Lord Jesus Christ, which was shed for thee, preserve thy soul unto everlasting life." [6]

The variation of these words in the order of "The Supper of the Lorde and the Holy Communion, Commonly Called the Masse," in the First Book of Common Prayer of 1549, is slight. They are: "The body of our Lord Jesus Christ which was given for thee, preserve thy body and soul unto everlasting life. . . . The blood of our Lord Jesus Christ which was shed for thee, preserve thy body and soul unto everlasting life." [7] In the prayer before the distribution the petition is made: "Grant us therefore (gracious Lord) so to eat the flesh of Thy dear Son Jesus Christ, and to drink His blood in these holy Mysteries, that we may continually dwell in Him, and He in us, that our sinful bodies may be made clean by His body, and our souls washed through His most precious blood." [8]

The Real Presence was the doctrine which formed the basis of the order set forth. It was the catholic doctrine as taught in the early church, the doctrine subscribed to also by the church of the Augsburg Confession. The English statements, however, lacked the Lutheran clarity that the Blessed Sacrament conveys forgiveness of sins by virtue of the atoning work of the Savior.

The ancient liturgies of the Western Church were used by

[6] "The Order of the Communion," *The Two Liturgies A. D. 1549 and A. D. 1552 with Other Documents Set Forth by Authority in the Reign of King Edward VI,* edited for the Parker Society by Joseph Ketley (Cambridge: The University Press, 1844), p. 8. Hereafter cited as *Two Liturgies.*

[7] Ibid., p. 92.

[8] Ibid. See also in the epiklesis, p. 88.

60

Cranmer in the compilation of the First Prayer Book. The old Latin services were simplified, condensed, and altered. The *Consultation* of Hermann von Wied continued to give liturgical guidance to Cranmer. The reform of the breviary by the Spaniard, Cardinal Quignon, was utilized. The *Brandenburg-Nurenberg Kirchenordnung,* a Lutheran work in which Osiander, the father-in-law of Cranmer, had had a hand, was utilized. It was conservative in its recommendations and in its theology.

It was too conservative to suit some of the English divines and most of the foreign theologians who had come to England at the invitation of Cranmer. They said that this First Prayer Book was too Lutheran. Cranmer himself had altered his position on the Real Presence. A commission was appointed to revise the Prayer Book; Parliament had passed an act which stated that the First Prayer Book was agreeable to the Word of God, but that doubts had arisen (through curiosity rather than any worthy cause), and it should be explained and made perfect.[9] The "explanation" resulted in an alteration or, as one editor put it, "a strong divergence from the principles which had marked the structure of the First Book."[10] There can be little question that the conscious attempt was made to get away from the medieval and Lutheran patterns that had been followed in the First Prayer Book.

This Second Prayer Book never came into general use. By law it was not to be put into use until 1 Nov. 1552. In July 1553, Mary, strong in her convictions and staunch in her adherence to the Roman Church, came to the throne. Mary did away with this liturgy. It was the basis, however, of the Elizabethan Prayer Book and for that reason must be examined more carefully.

[9] Leighton Pullan, *The History of the Book of Common Prayer;* 3d ed., 4th impression (London: Longmans, Green & Co., 1905), pp. 102—110.

[10] W. B., "Historical Introduction," *The Second Prayer Book of King Edward VI, 1552* (The Ancient and Modern Library of Theological Literature [London: Griffith, Farran, Okeden & Welsh, n.d.]), p. v. Cited as *Second P. B., 1552.*

Aidan Gasquet and Edmund Bishop, *Edward VI and the Book of Common Prayer,* rev. ed. (London: Sheed and Ward, 1928), have a detailed presentation. Dyson Hague, *Through the Prayer Book* (London: Church Book Room Press, Ltd., 1948), pp. 9—57.

Images had been removed from some of the churches. Ridley, as Bishop of Rochester and then Bishop of London, had ordered that the altars in the churches be replaced with tables. However, not all of the altars were removed. Vestments, too, had become a subject of controversy. The congregations of foreigners in London, especially that at which John a Lasco was minister, provided a pattern of a simple order of worship. The most violent objection was made to the rubric prescribing kneeling at the Holy Communion. While the Second Prayer Book was in print, the objections of John Knox prevailed with the Privy Council. Grafton, the printer, was ordered to insert a rubric which came to be known as the "Black Rubric." It read:

> Although no order can be so perfectly devised, but it may be of some, either for their ignorance and infirmity, or else of malice and obstinacy, misconstrued, depraved, and interpreted in a wrong part: And yet because brotherly charity willeth, that so much as conveniently may be, offences should be taken away: therefore we are willing to do the same. Whereas it is ordained in the Book of Common Prayer, in the administration of the Lord's Supper, that the communicants kneeling should receive the Holy Communion: which thing being well meant, for a signification of the humble and grateful acknowledging of the benefits of Christ, given unto the worthy receiver, and to avoid the profanation and disorder, which about the Holy Communion might else ensue: lest yet the same kneeling might be thought or taken otherwise, we do declare that it is not meant thereby, that any alteration be done, or ought to be done, either unto the sacramental bread or wine there bodily received or unto any real and essential presence there being of Christ's natural flesh and blood. For as concerning the sacramental bread and wine, they remain still in their very natural substances, and therefore may not be adored, for that were idolatry to be abhorred of all faithful Christians. And as concerning the natural body and blood of our Saviour Christ, they are in heaven and not here. For it is against the truth of Christ's true natural body, to be in more places than in one, at one time.[11]

[11] Ibid., p. 172; *Two Liturgies*, p. 283.

62

And so the Second Book of Common Prayer denied the Roman doctrine of transubstantiation, the Lutheran doctrine of the Real Presence, the Christology of the Lutheran divines (labeled "ubiquity" by the Reformed) and the ancient custom of kneeling.

In the distribution of the elements during the Holy Communion the minister said: "Take and eat this, in remembrance that Christ died for thee, and feed on Him in thy heart by faith, with thanksgiving. . . . Drink this in remembrance that Christ's blood was shed for thee, and be thankful." [12] These words in the Elizabethan Prayer Book could be taken in a Zwinglian sense, far removed from any Lutheran doctrine or the Roman teaching of the Mass.

Other changes were made in the Order of the Holy Communion. The Decalog and the Responses were added. The Introit was changed. The Prayer of Consecration, the Eucharistical Prayer, was altered. The epiklesis, or prayer for the elements, had been included in the First Book of Common Prayer by Cranmer, borrowed from the Eastern Liturgy of St. Basil. It read: "Hear us (O merciful Father) we beseech Thee; and with Thy Holy Spirit and Word, vouchsafe to bless and sanctify these Thy gifts, and creatures of bread and wine, that they may be unto us the body and blood of Thy most dearly beloved Son Jesus Christ." [13] The substitution read: "Hear us, O merciful Father, we beseech Thee; and grant that we, receiving these Thy creatures of bread and wine, according to Thy Son our Saviour Jesus Christ's holy institution, in remembrance of His death and passion, may be partakers of His most blessed body and blood." [14] It is no wonder that Anglo-Catholics decry the change!

In the Elizabethan Prayer Book the words of the altered epiklesis of the Second Prayer Book are retained. In the formula for the distribution of the elements in the Holy Supper the words of the First and the Second Prayer Book are combined, in an obvious compromise that might mean the Zwinglian view of a meal of

[12] *Second P. B., 1552*, p. 169; *Two Liturgies*, p. 279.

[13] *Two Liturgies*, p. 88.

[14] *Second P. B., 1552*, p. 169; *Two Liturgies*, p. 279.

commemoration, the Lutheran view of the Real Presence, or even the Roman view of the Substantial Presence:

The body of our Lord Jesu Christ, which was given for thee, preserve thy body and soul into everlasting life: and take and eat this in remembrance that Christ died for thee, feed on Him in thine heart by faith, with thanksgiving. . . . The blood of our Lord Jesu Christ, which was shed for thee, preserve thy body and soul into everlasting life; and drink this in remembrance that Christ's blood was shed for thee, and be thankful.[15]

The "Black Rubric" was not found in the Elizabethan Prayer Book.

The alterations in this prayer book were chiefly the work of Guest, archdeacon of Canterbury and later Bishop of Rochester. A committee, of course, had been entrusted with the task. William Cecil was a member of this commission, as was Matthew Parker; Francis Knollys and Francis Bacon both served as members of the Council. Ten points were of particular consequence, it seems, in the revisions that went into the Elizabethan Prayer Book. Strype gave them in the following form:

As first, Whether such ceremonies as were lately taken away by king Edward's book might not be resumed, not being evil in themselves?

II. Whether the image of the cross were not to be retained?

III. Whether processions should not be used?

IV. Whether in the celebration of the communion, priests should not use a cope beside a surplice?

V. Whether the communion should be divided into two parts? [that is, the office or book of communion.] And whether a part thereof should be read to all without distinction, and another to the communicants only, the rest being departed?

VI. Whether the creed is rightly placed in the communion office; as though it were to be repeated by the communicants only?

VII. Whether it is not convenient to continue praying for the dead in the communion?

---

[15] *Liturgical Services,* p. 195.

VIII. Whether the prayer of consecration in the first communion book should be left out?

IX. Whether the sacrament were, according to the first book, to be received into the communicant's mouth, or to be delivered into his hand?

X. Whether the sacrament were to be received standing or kneeling? [16]

The answers given to these questions by Guest show the thinking, in part, that went into the making of the Elizabethan Prayer Book. Ceremonies which once had been abolished, he held, ought not to be restored. However, the appearance of evil is to be avoided. Ceremonies become a burden, whereas the Gospel is the light and easy yoke; they might give occasion for idolatry. Guest did not wish to retain the image of the cross. Processions were superfluous, he held. The use of the surplice was sufficient also in the celebration of the Holy Communion. The Order of the Communion was divided into two parts in the ancient church. "To pray for the dead in the communion was not used in Christ and His apostles' time." He disliked the prayer in the first book for consecration, because it was thought to be needed for consecration; however, the petition actually was not part of the consecration. Then, too, he said, Christ, in instituting the Sacrament, made a prayer of thanksgiving but not of petition. He adduced arguments from Gregory, Chrysostom, Bessarion, and Justin. As for the manner of distributing the Sacrament, he wrote, Christ gave the bread into the hands of the disciples. It should be received standing rather than kneeling.[17]

The first rubric of the Elizabethan Prayer Book directed that matins and vespers, or morning and evening prayer, were to be used "in the accustomed place of the church, chapel, or chancel." "And here it is to be noted, that the Minister at the time of the communion, and at all other times in his ministration, shall use such ornaments in the church, as were in use by authority of Parliament

[16] Strype, *Elizabeth*, I, i, 120, 121.
[17] Ibid., I, ii, Appendix, No. XIV, pp. 459—464.

65

in the second year of the reign of Edward the VI. according to the act of Parliament set in the beginning of this book." [18] The nave might not be substituted for the chancel, nor were the rochet and the surplice to be the only vestments used in a chancel devoid of any ornamentation.

In the Litany, the words "from the tyranny of the bishop of Rome and all his detestable enormities" were omitted. The significance of this omission is clear only if it is regarded as an effort to remove a cause of offense to some of the queen's subjects. In the suffrage for the queen these words were added: "strengthen [her] in the true worshipping of Thee, in righteousness, and holiness of life." [19] The prayer for the queen and one for the clergy were added at the end of the Litany.

On 24 June 1559 the Act of Uniformity went into effect, and the Elizabethan Prayer Book was put into use.

Some of the rubrics of the Elizabethan Book of Common Prayer give an insight into the services held in the Elizabethan days. None of the rubrics prescribe that hymns should be sung. Hymn singing was introduced in September 1559 at St. Antholin's in London. Here the morning prayer included singing by the congregation, "when a psalm was sung after the Geneva fashion; all the congregation, men, women, and boys, singing together." [20] Immediately hymn singing became popular. A report in March 1560 stated:

Religion is now somewhat more established than it was. The people are every where exceedingly inclined to the better part. The practice of joining in church music has very much conduced to this. For as soon as they had once commenced singing in public, in one little church in London, immediately not only the churches in the neighbourhood, but even the towns far distant, began to vie with each other in the same practice. You may now sometimes see at Paul's cross, after the service, six thousand persons,

[18] *Liturgical Services,* p. 53.

[19] Ibid., pp. 12 f.

[20] Strype, *Elizabeth,* I, i, 199; see *Zurich Letters,* I (1558—1567), 33, n. 3

old and young, of both sexes, all singing together and praising God. This sadly annoys the mass-priests, and the devil.[21]

In the Morning Prayer the rubric provided: "And (to the end the people may the better hear) in such places where they do sing, there shall the lessons be sung in a plain tune after the manner of distinct reading: and likewise the Epistle and Gospel."[22] The Litany was read on Sundays, Wednesdays, and Fridays.

Holy Communion was celebrated only when there was "a good number to communicate with the priest." In small parishes, those with not more than twenty persons eligible for Communion, a minimum of three or four were to participate with the priest. In cathedral and collegiate churches all the priests and deacons were to receive Communion every Sunday. Easter Communion was made mandatory on all; three times was the minimum number of Communion attendances per year of anyone. Easter, too, was the day on which every parishioner should pay his ecclesiastical dues.

The bread used in the Holy Communion was ordinary bread. The rubric read: "And to take away the superstition, which any person hath, or might have in the bread and wine, it shall suffice that the bread be such as is usual to be eaten at the table, with other meats, but the best and purest wheat bread, that conveniently may be gotten." The curate and the churchwardens were to provide the bread and wine at the charge of the parish. If bread and wine remained after the celebration of the Holy Communion, "the curate shall have it to his own use."[23]

Public baptisms were administered on Sundays or holy days, "when the most number of people may come together, as well

21 John Jewel to Peter Martyr, London, 5 March 1560, *Zurich Letters,* I, 71.

Strype, *Elizabeth,* I, i, 297: "March 3rd [1560] . . . And after sermon a psalm was sung, (which was the common practice of the reformed churches abroad,) wherein the people also joined their voices."

Ibid., I, i, 298: "Ditto the 17th. . . . And after sermon done, they sung all in common a psalm in metre, as it seems now was frequently done, the custom being brought in from abroad by the exiles."

22 *Liturgical Services,* p. 57.

23 Ibid., p. 198.

for that the congregation there present may testify the receiving of them that be newly baptized into the number of Christ's church, as also because in the baptism of infants every man present may be put in remembrance of his own profession made to God in his baptism." [24] Emergency might well require that children be baptized at home, and this was allowed. The Puritans inveighed against this "women's baptism," but the Prayer Book provided a form "Of Them That Be Baptized in Private Houses in Time of Necessity." Pastors and curates were to admonish the people not to defer Baptism any longer than the Sunday or holy day immediately after the birth of the child or "without great cause and necessity" to baptize the children at home. [25] Dipping or pouring on of water was allowed either for public or for private Baptism.

Confirmation was restricted to those who were able to repeat in English the Apostles' Creed, the Lord's Prayer, and the Ten Commandments, and who could answer the questions of the Catechism. Confirmation, administered by a bishop, was the ratification of the promise by the godparents at the time of baptism. The imposition of hands and prayer were given for "strength and defence against all the temptations to sin, and the assaults of the world and the devil." [26] According to the usage of the church, confirmation was reserved for those who had been instructed, after they had attained the years of discretion, and who were ready to make profession of their faith and a promise of obedience to the will of God.

The Catechism did little more than rehearse the Creed, the Ten Commandments, and the Lord's Prayer. The teaching of justification was not omitted in the Catechism since Jesus is described as the Son of God, "who hath redeemed me and all mankind," but the teaching of sanctification was its prominent feature. Duty toward God was defined, in the answer of the catechumen, as ". . . to believe in Him, to fear Him, and to love Him with all my heart, with all my mind, with all my soul, and with all my strength. To worship Him. To give Him thanks. To put my whole

[24] Ibid., p. 199.

[25] Ibid., p. 206.

[26] Ibid., p. 210.

trust in Him. To call upon Him. To honor His holy name and His Word, to serve Him truly all the days of my life." [27] There are echoes of Luther's Small Catechism in this answer. These echoes were not quite so pronounced in the summary of the duties toward the neighbor.

My duty towards my neighbor is to love him as myself: And to do to all men as I would they should do unto me. To love, honour, and succour [help] my father and mother. To honour and obey the Kyng, and his ministers [an obvious misprint for "the Queen and her ministers"]. To submit myself to all my governors, teachers, spiritual Pastors and masters. To order myself lowly and reverently to all my betters. To hurt nobody by word, nor deed. To be true and just in all my dealing. To bear no malice nor hatred in my heart. To keep my hands from picking and stealing, and my tongue from evil speaking, lying and slandering. To keep my body in temperance, soberness, and chastity. Not to covet nor desire other men's goods. But learn and labour truly to get mine own living, and to do my duty in that state of life, unto which it shall please God to call me.[28]

The solemnization of matrimony required the prior publication of banns in the parishes of both contracting parties. Marriages were to be solemnized in church. The form provided for the use of the ring. This, too, became a point of contention for the Puritans, as did the words which the man repeated: "With this ring I thee wed: with my body I thee worship: and with all my worldly goods, I thee endow." [29] A Communion service was held in connection with the wedding. The rubric provided, "The new married persons (the same day of their marriage) must receive the Holy Communion." [30]

The importance given to the Holy Communion can be seen also from the fact that a form was provided for the Communion of the sick in addition to the form for the visitation of the sick.

[27] Ibid., p. 211.
[28] Ibid., p. 213.
[29] Ibid., p. 219.
[30] Ibid., p. 224.

The rubric directed the curate to exhort the parishioners to receive the Holy Communion diligently, especially "in the plague time," so that they might be ready to die. If a sick person wished Holy Communion, it was to be given to him. A "good number" was to receive the Communion with the sick person; at times of plague or times of other contagious diseases, when none of the parish would commune with the sick person, "for fear of the infection," the Holy Eucharist might be administered to the sick person alone. Even in the administration of the Holy Communion to the sick the minister was to commune himself first. What consolation could be given to a sick person who for some reason could not receive or could not be given Holy Communion, "the Sacrament of Christ's body and blood"? He was to be instructed that "if he do truly repent him of his sins, and stedfastly believe that Jesus Christ has suffered death upon the cross for him, and shed His blood for his redemption, earnestly remembering the benefits he hath thereby, and giving Him hearty thanks therefor, he doth eat and drink the body and blood of our Saviour Christ, profitably to his soul's health, although he do not receive the Sacrament with his mouth." [31]

Holy Communion, too, was to be received by a woman who came to church to give thanks after childbirth, "if there be a Communion." [32]

The Ordinal, printed separately from the Book of Common Prayer, provided for the ordaining of deacons, priests, bishops, and archbishops. In each instance a bishop [or archbishop] was to perform the rite. Deacons had to be at least twenty years of age for ordination; priests, twenty-four; bishops, thirty. The qualifications, in terms of character and godly life, were set high. With the ordination rite the Holy Communion was celebrated. The "Oath of the Queen's Sovereignty" was administered to the candidate, in which he acknowledged her as the only supreme governor of the realm "as well in all spiritual or ecclesiastical things or causes." [33]

[31] Ibid., p. 232.
[32] Ibid., p. 238.
[33] Ibid., pp. 272—298.

The Book of Common Prayer did not give a prominent place to the sermon. Scripture readings and lections were provided for in abundance — this may be counted a strong point of the Anglican ritual. In the Order for the Holy Communion the rubric provided, "After the Creed if there be no sermon, shall follow one of the Homilies already set forth, or hereafter to be set forth by common authority." [34] The Puritans, it may be remarked, found fault later with the "dumb reading" of the Scriptures, the reading without comment, with the reading of the Homilies, and the lack of sermons. The sermon did not receive the same emphasis in the Anglican reform as it had in the Lutheran and Swiss prototypes. In this respect it remained closer to the medieval pattern.

The Book of Common Prayer provided for the observance of holy days. The cycle of the church year was followed. Accordingly the ecclesiastical year began with the Sundays of Advent, four Sundays before Christmas. After Christmas there were one or two Sundays, and then the Sundays after Epiphany, which might number as many as five. Three Sundays preceded Lent: Septuagesima, Sexagesima, and Quinquagesima. The six Sundays of Lent were followed by Easter. Five Sundays after Easter and the Sunday after Ascension preceded Whitsunday. Then came Trinity Sunday and the Sundays after Trinity, perhaps as many as twenty-six. Within this cycle of the church year the holy days were fixed. These according to the calendar year were:

January 1	Circumcision
January 6	Epiphany
January 25	Conversion of St. Paul
February 2	Purification of Mary
February 24	St. Matthias
March 25	The Annunciation
April 23	St. George
April 25	St. Mark the Evangelist
May 1	St. Philip and St. James
June 11	Barnabas the Apostle
June 24	The Nativity of John the Baptist
June 29	St. Peter the Apostle

[34] Ibid., p. 183.

71

July 25	St. James the Apostle
August 10	St. Laurence
August 24	St. Bartholomew the Apostle
September 21	St. Matthew
September 29	St. Michael and All Angels
October 18	St. Luke the Evangelist
October 28	St. Simon and St. Jude
November 1	All Saints' Day
November 23	St. Clement
November 30	St. Andrew the Apostle
December 21	St. Thomas the Apostle
December 25	Christmas, the Feast of the Nativity
December 26	St. Stephen
December 27	St. John the Evangelist
December 28	The Holy Innocents

Certain days did not fall on a fixed calendar day. These were the Wednesday before Easter, the Thursday before Easter, Good Friday, and Easter Eve. So they were designated. Ash Wednesday at the beginning of Lent was not listed. The Monday and Tuesday in Easter week were. Ascension Day, forty days after Easter, had its place in the church calendar. The Monday and the Tuesday in Whitsun week were observed.[35]

There were thirty-six holy days, including Easter and Pentecost, besides the other fifty Sundays in the year. No month was without its holy day. Easter would usually fall between the 25th of March and the 25th of April; Ascension and Whitsuntide, between the 1st of May and the 11th of June.

In the Elizabethan Prayer Book a short treatise "Of Ceremonies, Why Some Be Abolished, and Some Retained" was found. It spoke of holy days and ceremonies. "In this our time," it said, there were many different beliefs; some individuals as a matter of conscience wanted no change; some "be so new fangled" they wanted complete innovations. The Prayer Book aimed at pleasing God, the treatise stated, and so would profit the extremists on both sides. Some ceremonies were abolished because they had become burdensome. Moreover, Christ's Gospel, it stated, "is a religion to serve

[35] Ibid., pp. 38—52.

72

God, not in bondage of the figure, or shadow, but in the freedom of spirit." Some ceremonies were abolished because of the abuses connected with them. Those that were retained were retained for discipline and order, and might be changed, since they were not equal to God's Law. "And moreover they be neither dark nor dumb ceremonies, but are so set forth, that every man may understand what they do mean, and to what use they do serve." Finally, these doings did not imply the condemnation of some other people's observances. "For we think it convenient that every country should use such ceremonies, as they shall think best, to the setting forth of God's honour, or glory, and to the reducing of the people to a most perfect and godly living, without error or superstition." [36]

[36] Ibid., p. 38.

CHAPTER V

THE CLERGY AND THE ELIZABETHAN
SETTLEMENT

ishops were part of the religious scene in England throughout the Middle Ages and were retained by the religious settlements of Henry VIII, Edward VI, and Elizabeth. Only the relatively brief years of the Puritan regime in the seventeenth century did not have them. There seems to have been no question in the mind of Elizabeth about the retention of the episcopate.

In addition to the archbishops of Canterbury and York there were twenty-four bishops in the realm. However, ten sees were vacant on 8 May 1559, the day the Act of Uniformity and the Act of Supremacy received the royal assent. The administration of the church and the establishment of the Religious Settlement required the appointment of new bishops and the compliance of the old bishops. In Parliament they had voted against all bills dealing with the Religious Settlement. Their general refusal to crown the queen and even their conduct at the Westminster Disputation would count against them. "The bishops were on the spot to be bent or broken." [1]

A week after the adjournment of Parliament the sixteen bishops were in the presence of the queen, summoned there to swear allegiance to her as Supreme Governor of the Church of England.

[1] Froude, *History of England,* VII, 91.

75

Nicholas Heath, the archbishop of York, as the highest-ranking prelate present, gave the answer for all of them, asking Elizabeth to return to the Church of Rome and to acknowledge the headship of the pope.

A commission of eighteen was appointed on the 23d of May to administer the oath to all officials of whom it was required. The bishops were the first ones who were requested to subscribe. Fifteen of the sixteen refused. Anthony Kitchin, bishop of Llandaff in Wales, was the only bishop to take the oath.[2]

Some in these days of the religious change, as may be gathered from the incidental remarks of a returned exile, reviled the old bishops:

The pope is again cast out of England. This sadly annoys the mass-mongers. The pseudo-bishops opposed with all their might the pious designs of the queen; and, to be brief, brought upon themselves a consummation much desired by all good men. They are now abhorred both by God and man, and never creep out into public unless they are compelled to do so, lest perchance a tumult should arise among the people. Many call them *butchers* to their face.[3]

There was no great eagerness to replace the bishops in the vacant sees. Months after Parliament had enacted the religious change an impatient Protestant divine wrote:

[2] Hughes, *Reformation in England*, III, 56, n. 3, remarked: "We do not know the date on which Antony Kitchin of Llandaff took the oath, nor indeed that he ever took it. . . ." Others, e. g., F. L. Cross, ed. *The Oxford Dictionary of the Christian Church* (London: Oxford University Press, 1957), sub "Llandaff," p. 816, said he took the oath but gave no date.

J. C. Whitebrook, *The Consecration of the Most Reverend Matthew Parker, Archbishop of Canterbury Effected by the Rt. Rev. Anthony Kitchin* (London and Oxford: A. R. Mowbray & Co., Ltd., 1945), 21, maintained that Kitchin did not conform. His thesis, p. 112, that Kitchin "plainly planned, and failed to achieve . . . to preserve a corner of England, with a validly ordained priesthood, ready for reunion with the Catholic Church," needs more documentary proof than he has brought.

[3] John Parkhurst to Conrad Gesner, London, 21 May 1559, *Zurich Letters*, I (1558—79), No. 13, p. 31.

There seems to be far too much prudence, too much mystery, in the management of these affairs; and God alone knows what will be the issue. The slow-paced horses retard the chariot. . . . The bishops are as yet only marked out [for promotion], and their estates are in the mean time gloriously swelling the exchequer.[4]

The moneys accruing to the royal treasury from the vacant bishoprics hindered the establishment of a full ecclesiastical administration. "The Act for the Restitution of the First Fruits and Tenths, and Rents reserved *Nomine Decimae,* and of Parsonages Impropriate, to the Imperial Crown of this Realm," and particularly "The Act, giving Authority to the Queen's Majesty upon the Avoidance of any Archbishoprick or Bishoprick, to take into Her Hands certain of the Temporal Possessions thereof, recompensing the same with Parsonages Impropriate and Tenths,"[5] gave the queen and her courtiers "a fair opportunity to pick and choose what houses, lands, and revenues they pleased." The protests of Parker and others, mild as they had to be,[6] did not deter this impoverishment of the clergy. Richard Cox protested that "kings and queens shall be patrons and nurses [not spoilers and stepdames] of his church and people." He realized the royal need for money, but the queen should not burden her conscience by the spoliation of the church nor forget the needs of the parishes.[7]

[4] John Jewel to Peter Martyr, London, 16 Nov. 1559, ibid., I (1558 to 1579), No. 24, p. 55.

[5] *L. J.,* I, 579; *Calendar of State Papers, Domestic Series, of the Reigns of Edward VI., Mary, Elizabeth, 1547—80,* preserved in the State Paper Department of her majesty's Public Record Office, ed. Robert Lemon (London: Longman, Brown, Green, Longman, & Robert, 1956), 127 (vol. iv, No. 2). Cited as *Dom. Cal., 1547—80.*

[6] Archbishop Parker, elect, and four other bishops elect, to Queen Elizabeth, ca. 15 Oct. 1559, *Correspondence of Matthew Parker,* edited for the Parker Society by John Bruce and Thomas T. Perowne (Cambridge: The University Press, 1853), No. LXVIII, pp. 97—101. Cited as *Parker's Correspondence.*

[7] Strype, *Elizabeth,* I, i, 142—147. See also Peter Heylyn, *Ecclesia Restaurata; or, The History of the Church of England,* ed. James C. Robertson (Ecclesiastical History Society edition; Cambridge: The University Press, 1849), II, 307, 308. Also John Strype, *The Life and Acts of Matthew Parker,* new ed. (Oxford: The Clarendon Press, 1821), I, 88—90; II, Appendix X.

The most important vacancy was the Archbishopric of Canterbury, for Reginald Cardinal Pole had died the same day on which Queen Mary died. Elizabeth appointed Matthew Parker to this post.

Matthew Parker had attended the University of Cambridge, where he was a Fellow of Corpus Christi College and then Master. He may have been a member of the "White Horse" group, the "Germans" at Cambridge in the 1520s who gathered to study the writings of Martin Luther.[8] His sympathy with Thomas Bilney led him to be present at the burning of Bilney at Norwich on 19 Aug. 1531. Parker has been called the disciple of Dr. Robert Barnes, "Luther's English friend." Later Martin Bucer influenced his thinking; he preached the sermon at Bucer's funeral.[9] Thomas Cranmer exercised a great influence on him.

Parker, ordained in 1527, was called to the court as chaplain to Queen Anne [Boleyn] in 1533 or 1534, and in 1537 he was made chaplain to King Henry VIII. He received his doctor of divinity degree in 1538, at the age of thirty-four. He had various preferences. Twice he was elected Vice-Chancellor of Cambridge [in 1545 and in 1549]. In July 1552 he became Dean of Lincoln.

At the beginning of Queen Mary's reign he was deprived of his various offices; he remained, however, in England and did not, like others, flee to the Continent. "After this I lived," he himself wrote of this period, "as a private individual, so happy before God in my conscience, and so far from being either ashamed or dejected, that the delightful literary leisure to which the good providence of God recalled me yielded me much greater and more solid enjoyments, than my former busy and dangerous kind of life had ever afforded."[10] Industrious, conscientious, devoted, he preferred the sedentary life of a student and writer to the active life of an administrator, sharing the sentiments of Calvin and Melanchthon in this

[8] E. G. Rupp, *Studies in the Making of the English Protestant Tradition* (Cambridge: The University Press, 1914), p. 29; Porter, *Tudor Cambridge*, p. 47.

[9] Ibid., pp. 67—70. Walter F. Hook, *Lives of the Archbishops of Canterbury* (London: Richard Bentley & Son, 1872), IX, 35—44.

[10] *Parker's Correspondence*, p. viii.

respect. During these years of retirement he completed a metrical version of the Psalter in English and wrote a defense of the marriage of priests — he himself was married.

Throughout his life Parker continued his interest in collecting manuscripts. Among his writings is his *De antiquitate ecclesiae et privilegiis ecclesiae cantuariensis cum archiepiscopis eius lxx.* He became the first publisher of materials for English history.[11] The services he rendered in preserving manuscripts are still valued highly by scholars.[12] A similar high regard brought about the formation of the Parker Society in 1840 "for the publication of the fathers, and early writers of the Reformed English Church." [13] Parker died in 1575 at the age of seventy-one.[14]

Parker was Archbishop of Canterbury for fifteen years. His part in the actual making of the Elizabethan Religious Settlement was not a significant one; he was made responsible for seeing that it was put into effect. Although he had been appointed to the commission to review the Prayer Book, the state of his health did not permit him to take an active part in this work (from February to the end of April 1559).[15]

Within three weeks after the accession of Elizabeth he was summoned to London for an interview, already singled out for the metropolitanship.[16] All he wanted for himself, however, was the revenue of some prebend; he had hoped to serve perhaps in a simple parish, or better yet, "of all places in England," in the University of Cambridge. "But to tell you my heart, I had rather have such a thing as Benet College is in Cambridge, a living of

[11] Ibid., p. xiii. Strype, *Matthew Parker,* II, 497—523.

[12] See, e. g., Richard Vaughan, *Matthew Paris* (Cambridge: The University Press, 1958), p. 180; Porter, *Tudor Cambridge,* p. 90.

[13] George Stokes' heirs were proud that he was the founder of the Parker Society and had his bookplates tell of this service.

[14] Strype's *Matthew Parker* is the fullest account of the life of the archbishop. All subsequent accounts are based to a great extent on Strype.

[15] Strype, *Matthew Parker,* I, 70.

[16] Sir Nicholas Bacon to Dr. Matthew Parker, 9 Dec. 1558, *Parker's Correspondence,* No. XL, p. 49.

twenty nobles by the year at the most, than to dwell in the deanery of Lincoln, which is two hundred at the least." [17] He recognized the importance of the office and the need for a man with the highest qualifications. "God grant," he had written to Bacon, "it chanceth neither on arrogant man, neither on fainthearted man, nor on covetous man." For one thing, this man should do nothing that "shall discourage his fellows to join him in unity of doctrine, which must be their whole strength." [18] He had no ambitions for that office; his poverty and a physical infirmity alike made him unsuitable, he felt, for the office. He was willing to serve anywhere except in the archbishopric.[19] Eventually he wrote to Elizabeth herself, begging to be excused from assuming that position, which, he said, required "a man of much more wit, learning, virtue, and experience," than he possessed.[20] Parker's sincerity in his protestations need not be questioned; he was modest; he desired a life of literary labors. However, in many respects he was well qualified for this office because of his training, intellectual ability, and past experience. He was wise, pious, kind, grave, discreet, modest, moderate; he "had in him an admirable mixture of gravity and honesty, learning and prudence, gentleness and obliging behavior." [21] The insistence of the queen enforced by Sir Nicholas Bacon and Sir William Cecil, forced Parker eventually to accept the highest ecclesiastical position in the realm.[22]

In the interval Elizabeth's officials did not hesitate to use Parker in various capacities. He was called on for advice, as noted above,

[17] Dr. Matthew Parker to Sir Nicholas Bacon, Dec. 1558, ibid., No. XLI, p. 51.

[18] Dr. Matthew Parker to Sir Nicholas Bacon, 1 March 1559, ibid., No. XLVI, p. 57.

[19] Ibid., pp. 58—63.

[20] Dr. Matthew Parker to Queen Elizabeth, June 1559, ibid., No. LIV, pp. 69, 70.

[21] Strype, *Matthew Parker,* I, 71.

[22] Sir William Cecil to Dr. Matthew Parker, Westminster, 30 Dec. 1558, ibid., No. XLIII, p. 53; Sir Nicholas Bacon to Dr. Matthew Parker, 4 Jan. 1559, ibid., No. XLIV, p. 53; Sir Nicholas Bacon to Dr. Matthew Parker, 17 May 1559, ibid., No. LI, p. 68; Strype, *Matthew Parker,* I, 71—79.

for the revision of the Prayer Book, although his part in this work was very small. He gave advice about the proper method of electing and consecrating bishops, noting that the Ordinal of Edward VI's reign would have to be used, "for there is none other especially made in this last session of Parliament."[23] He informed William Cecil, who was also Chancellor of Cambridge University, of conditions within the University, advising a visitation.[24] Cecil used him to settle various matters at the University.[25]

The formal details of the election procedure have been preserved for us. On 18 July 1559 the queen issued the letters patent, the *congé d' élire,* for the election.[26] The order for the consecration was drawn up at the same time.[27] On the 1st of August the Dean, Dr. Nicholas Wotton, and four canons met — seven were absent — for the election. They decided to proceed in the election by way and form of compromise; Dean Wotton was elected as compromissory. Parker was properly notified of his election and accepted it; the queen certified and confirmed it.[28]

On the 9th of September the queen issued letters patent to Bishop Tunstall and five others, commanding them to consecrate Matthew Parker as Archbishop of Canterbury.[29] Tunstall was not ready to perform this act. Then, too, Parker and several bishops remained unconsecrated because "the exchange between the Crown and them for certain temporalities has not been effected."[30] Per-

[23] Ibid., I, 81.

[24] Dr. Matthew Parker to Sir William Cecil, Cambridge, 1 March 1559, *Parker's Correspondence,* No. XLV, pp. 54—56. Strype, *Matthew Parker,* I, 82, 83.

[25] *Parker's Correspondence,* Nos. XLVII, XLVIII, pp. 63—65; No. L, p. 67; Nos. LVI, LVII, LVIII, LIX, pp. 71—74.

[26] Strype, *Matthew Parker,* I, 102.

[27] *Dom. Cal.,* 1547—80, p. 135 (vol. v, No. 24).

[28] Strype, *Matthew Parker,* I, 107.

[29] *Dom. Cal.,* 1547—80, p. 139 (vol. vi, No. 41); *Calendar of Patent Rolls Preserved in the Public Record Office, Elizabeth* (London: His Majesty's Stationery Office, 1939), I (1558—60), 28. Cited as *Cal. Patent Rolls, Eliz.,* I (1558—60).

[30] Ibid., p. 141 (vol. vii, No. 19).

haps there was a question of the validity of this directive. When the letters patent were issued on the 6th of December an attestation of Dr. William May and others was added that it was of sufficient force for the purpose.[31] It contained the *supplentes* paragraph, which stated:

> *Supplying* nevertheless by our supreme authority royal of our mere motion and certain knowledge, if any thing be or shall be wanting, either in the things, which according to our foresaid commandment shall be done, or in you or any of you, by reason of your condition, state, or power, to perform the premises; anything, I say, required or necessary in this behalf, either by the statutes of this our kingdom, or by the ecclesiastical laws, the circumstances of time, or the necessity of things requiring it.[32]

On that same day, the 6th of December, royal assent was given to the consecration of Parker as Archbishop of Canterbury.[33] The confirmation took place on the 9th of December in St. Mary le Bow Church.[34] On the 17th of December, Matthew Parker was consecrated in Lambeth Chapel. William Barlow, John Scory, who also preached the installation sermon, Myles Coverdale, and John Hodgkins participated in the solemn rite.[35] Neither Matthew Parker nor the queen nor others were concerned that he be consecrated in "Apostolic Succession." He was consecrated by bishops because

[31] Ibid., p. 143 (vol. vii, No. 56); *Cal. Patent Rolls, Eliz.,* I (1558 to 1560), 449, 450.

[32] Strype, *Matthew Parker,* I, 108.

[33] *Dom. Cal.,* 1547—80, p. 143 (vol. viii, No. 57).

[34] Strype, *Matthew Parker,* I, 107—110.

[35] *Dom. Cal.,* 1547—80, p. 144 (vol. vii, No. 67), 17 Dec. 1559, "Memorandum of the Consecration of Archb. Parker"; No. 68, 17 Dec. 1559, "Relation of the rites and ceremonies used at the consecration and installation of Matthew Parker, Archbishop of Canterbury"; No. 69 (copy of the above); Strype, *Matthew Parker,* I, 113—116.

Parker himself attested to this date. *Parker's Correspondence,* p. viii.

Other contemporary evidence is at hand. *Machyn's Diary,* p. 220.

Whitebrook, *Consecration of Matthew Parker,* discounts the evidence of the Lambeth Register, Parker's own testimony, and Machyn's entry.

Strype, *Matthew Parker,* I, 117—123, refutes the Nag's Head fable.

of the dignity of the office, not because of the necessity of keeping a direct continuity. Apostolic succession became the concern of churchmen of a later generation.

Parker said nothing about apostolic succession in a letter to Nicholas Heath. Heath had written to Parker and the bishops of the English Church, demanding that they acknowledge the primacy of Rome. In his answer Parker said:

> . . . whereas you and the rest of the late expulsed bishops have scandalized our reformed clergy within these her Majesty's realms, that we yield no subjection unto Christ and His Apostles, we yield more than ye fathers of the Romish tribe do; for we honor and adore Christ as the true Son of God, equal with His Father as well in authority as in majesty, and do make Him no foreigner to the realm, as you members and clergy of the church of Rome do; but we profess Him to be our only Maker and Redeemer, and Ruler of His Church, not only in this realm, but also in all nations, unto whom princes and preachers are but servants; the preachers to propose, the princes to execute, Christ's will and commandments, whom you, and all that desire to be saved, must believe and obey, against all councils and tribunals who do dissent from His word, whether regal or papal.

He professed reverence for the apostles, whose word he received as the Word of God; he denied the Petrine claims of the papacy, citing the examples of Cyprian and Augustine. He repudiated the unlawful demands of the bishops of Rome. "We are sorry," he wrote, "that ye have separated yourselves not only from us, but from these ancient fathers and their opinions; . . . What was it occasioned the Romish writers to write against the Bishop of Rome? What was it caused Luther, Calvin, and other orthodox clergymen, to renounce Rome and her church, but this thing called the bishop of Rome's tribunal?" [36]

On 17 Dec. 1559, the date on which Matthew Parker was consecrated as Archbishop of Canterbury, the following took the oath

[36] Archbishop Parker to Dr. Nicholas Heath, deprived Archbishop of York, and other deprived bishops, 26 March 1560, *Parker's Correspondence*, No. LXXVII, pp. 109—113.

to the queen (the sees in which they were to serve are appended to their names): Edmund Grindal, bishop of London; Richard Cox, bishop of Ely; William Barlow, bishop of Chichester; John Scory, bishop of Hereford; Edwin Sandys, bishop of Worcester, later archbishop of York; Roland Merick, bishop of Bangor; Nicholas Bolingham, bishop of Lincoln; John Jewel, bishop of Salisbury; Thomas Young, bishop of St. David's; Richard Davis, bishop of St. Asaph.[37] Grindal, Cox, Sandys, and Merick were consecrated on 21 Dec. 1559 by Archbishop Parker, assisted by Bishops Barlow, Scory, and Hodgkins. On 21 Jan. 1560 Young, Bolingham, Jewel, Davis, and Guest (as bishop of Rochester), were consecrated. On 2d of March, Pilkington (as bishop of Durham), and John Best (as bishop of Carlisle), on the 24th of March Will Barkley (as bishop of Bath and Wells) and John Bentham (as bishop of Litchfield and Coventry) were consecrated. Seven sees remained to be filled; of these the most important one was the Archbishopric of York. Dean William May had been elected to this post, but died on 12 Aug. 1560, before his consecration.[38]

Strype said of these bishops: "These were men worthy of their episcopal dignity; being all endued with learning and piety, and that had been exiles and confessors for the true religion; those qualifications being chiefly regarded in this choice, rather than either high birth, wealth, or other worldly consideration." [39] The youngest of them was forty (both Grindal and Jewel were of that age); the oldest were sixty, Barlow and Cox having attained that

[37] Thomas Sampson to Peter Martyr, 6 Jan. 1560, *Zurich Letters,* I (1558—79), No. XXVII, p. 63: "The consecration of some bishops has already taken place. I mention, as being known to you by name, Dr. Parker [archbishop] of Canterbury, Cox [bishop] of Ely, Grindal of London, Sandys of Worcester. There is one other of the name of Barlowe, also a bishop, but with whom you are not acquainted. Pilkington [bishop-elect] of Winchester, Bentham of Coventry, and your friend Jewel of Salisbury, will follow shortly; . . ." He was not accurate in reporting about Pilkington.
Strype, *Matthew Parker,* I, 124 f.

[38] Ibid., I, 126—128; Hughes, *Reformation in England,* III, 44, 45; Strype, *Elizabeth,* I, i, 230

[39] Strype, *Matthew Parker,* I, 128.

dignity. Their average age was forty-nine. Twelve of these men had been on the Continent, exiles during the reign of Queen Mary. The vast majority of them had held administrative positions of trust in the universities of England.[40] Most of them were moderate men. In general, those who had been in exile were more inclined toward Calvinism than the others. The question of episcopacy verses presbyterianism was not yet an issue. Some of these men were ready to assume the episcopal office so that they might advance the more radical reformation. Such a rationalization consoled Peter Martyr, who had not been appointed bishop:

> But though I have always been opposed to ornaments of this kind [vestments], yet as I perceived the present danger of your being deprived of the office of preaching, and that there will perhaps be some hope that, like as altars and images have been removed, so the resemblance of the mass may also be taken away, provided you and others who may obtain bishopricks, will direct all your endeavours to that object, (which should make less progress, should another succeed in your place, who not only might be indifferent about putting away those relics, but would rather defend, cherish, and maintain them;) therefore was I slower in advising you rather to refuse a bishoprick, than to consent to the use of those garments.[41]

A few of these men were regarded as Puritans later. Most of them were content to follow the *via media*. One of them has been classified as a Lutheran, Richard Cheney, in 1553 Archdeacon of Hereford and in 1562 made Bishop of Gloucester; he had, said Hughes, "the distinction of being the solitary Lutheran among these bishops."[42] Among all the bishops there were very few

[40] Porter, *Tudor Cambridge*, pp. 81, 88.

[41] Peter Martyr to Thomas Sampson, Zurich, 4 Nov. 1559, *Zurich Letters*, II (1558—1602), No. XIV, pp. 32, 33.

[42] Hughes, *Reformation in England*, III, 46; Strype, *Elizabeth*, I, i, 420, remarked of Cheney that he was "as Camden saith of him, most addicted to Luther, both in respect, I suppose, of the doctrine of the presence, as also for the retaining of old customs, as crucifixes and pictures of saints in the churches, and such like." See also Rowse, *The England of Elizabeth*, pp. 415 f.

outstanding theologians. John Jewel was the pre-eminent theologian among them.

John Jewel, a close friend of Peter Martyr, was one of the very important Reformed theologians of the period [43] and one of the intellectual leaders of the Elizabethan church. His controversy with Thomas Harding brought on the publication of his *Apologia ecclesiae anglicanae*. His inclinations were toward the spiritual aspects of his office, "attending to the flock of Christ," as he himself remarked, rather than to its temporal and civil aspects, "royal pomp and courtly bustle." [44] He "administered his diocese with a vigour unusual in the Elizabethan Church, made several visitations, preached frequently, and built the library of Salisbury Cathedral." [45] Grindal paid Jewel the perfect tribute when he wrote about his death: "The excellent Bishop Jewel, of Salisbury, (the Jewel and singular ornament of the Church, as his name implies,) we lost, or rather I should say, sent before us, about the beginning of October last" [23 Sept. 1571].[46]

Grindal himself was one of the more noteworthy bishops appointed early in the reign of Elizabeth. He was chaplain to Edward VI, prebendary of Westminster, exile in Frankfurt, Bishop of London (1559), Archbishop of York (1570), Archbishop of Canterbury (1575). His difficulties with the queen, because of his refusal to suppress the Puritan prophesyings, do not belong to the story of the Elizabethan Settlement. His theology does. He was a moderate Calvinist who had a high regard for Luther. After disparaging those who "all but regard [Luther] as a god," he remarked: "Luther has indeed deserved exceeding well of the

[43] Joseph C. McLelland, *The Visible Words of God: An Exposition of the Sacramental Theology of Peter Martyr Vermigli, A.D. 1500—62* (Grand Rapids, Mich.: Wm. B. Eerdmans Publishing Co., 1957), 67, called him "one of the greatest of the Reformers."

[44] John Jewel to Josiah Simler, London, 2 Nov. 1559, *Zurich Letters*, I (1558—79), No. XXII, p. 51.

[45] F. L. Cross, ed. *The Oxford Dictionary of the Christian Church*, p. 726.

[46] Archbishop Grindal to Henry Bullinger, Bishopsthorpe, near York, 25 Jan. 1572, *Zurich Letters*, I (1558—79), No. C, p. 260.

church, and is worthy of being celebrated by all posterity."[47] He owned a set of Luther's works.[48] "His well known piety and learning"[49] recommended him not only to the queen but also to the foreigners who again established their Protestant churches in London.[50] Grindal deserves to be more highly regarded today than he is.

There are others among these bishops of whom the same can be said. They were secondary figures, but they had significant positions in the church. William Barlow, a former Augustinian, who in his *Dialogue* (1531) wrote against Luther, had held bishoprics in the time of Henry VIII and Edward VI. John Scory, too, had been a bishop during Edward's reign. Both men were capable theologians and administrators. Both had been buffeted by the years of exile; both were too little concerned with their pastoral responsibilities. Another, Richard Cox, is better known than they because of his involvement in the troubles at Frankfurt. The "Coxians" were named after him in the dispute with the "Knoxians," the followers of John Knox. The distinction of causing the controversy about the crucifix in the queen's chapel[51] does not make him the greatest exponent of Puritanism among the Elizabethan bishops. This distinction belongs to Edwin Sandys. Sandys, however, was not a forceful leader, nor was he associated closely with Puritanism as an organized movement. James Pilkington, too, favored more radical changes; yet he cannot be called a Puritan. His exposition of books of the Old Testament, especially Haggai

[47] Bishop Grindal to Conrad Hubert, London, 6 June 1562, *Zurich Letters*, II (1558—1602), No. XXXI, p. 73.

[48] Edmund Grindal to Conrad Hubert, London, 14 July 1559, ibid., No. X, p. 24.

[49] Conrad Hubert to Thomas Blaurer, Strassburgh, 7 Aug. 1559, ibid., No. XII, p. 27.

[50] Strype, *Elizabeth*, I, i, 174.

[51] John Jewel to Peter Martyr, London, 4 Feb. 1560, *Zurich Letters*, I (1558—79), No. XXIX, pp. 67, 68; cf. p. 66 n; Bishop Cox to George Cassander, London, 4 March 1560, ibid., II (1558—1602), No. XVIII, pp. 41, 42; George Cassander to Bishop Cox [Worms, 1560], No. XIX, pp. 42—47; Strype, *Elizabeth*, I, i, 259—261.

and Nehemiah, put him among the scholarly bishops. Edmund Guest, too, was a scholar. He had published *A Treatise against the Privy Mass* (1548) in the dispute about the Real Presence. Guest was influenced in part by Martin Luther in his opposition to the Zwinglian and Calvinistic doctrines.

Among the bishops of the early years of Elizabeth's reign these men stand out as leaders distinguished for learning and ability, training and character, integrity and moderation. But the seven thousand or more parish priests, rectors, ministers, curates, or pastors were closest to the people and most directly shaped their spiritual lives. During the Marian reaction some of them had gone back to Romanism. The stauncher Protestants, especially among the returned exiles, deplored the deficiencies among the ministers. "We are labouring under a great dearth of godly ministers: for many, who have fallen off in this persecution, are now papists in heart; and those who had been heretofore, so to speak, *moderate* papists, are now the most obstinate." [52] Few of the priests had ever preached the Gospel of Christ. [53] Peter Martyr spoke of the "great want of ministers" in England, fearing that the churches would become destitute of pastors or fall prey to "wolves and anti-Christs." [54] Jewel complained:

> For we have at this time not only to contend with our adversaries, but even with those of our friends who, of late years, have fallen away from us, and gone over to the opposite party; and who are now opposing us with a bitterness and obstinacy far exceeding that of any common enemy; and, what is most vexatious, we have to struggle with what has been left us by the Spaniards, that is, with the foulest vices, pride, luxury, and licentiousness. [55]

[52] Edmund Grindal to Conrad Hubert, London, 23 May 1559, *Zurich Letters,* II (1558—1602), No. VIII, p. 19.

[53] Thomas Lever to Henry Bullinger, London, 8 Aug. 1559, ibid., No. XIII, p. 31.

[54] Peter Martyr to [Thomas Sampson], Zurich, 1 Feb. 1560, ibid., No. XVII, p. 38.

[55] John Jewel to Henry Bullinger, London, 22 May 1559, ibid., I (1558—79), No. XIV, p. 32.

Jewel also wrote: "The existing preachers, who are few in number, those especially who have any ability, are listened to by the people with favour and attention." [56] Partisans viewed conditions in England according to their own predilections; however, the visitations made evident the need for a more fully trained ministry.

The need is brought out most tellingly by Archbishop Parker in a letter to the Bishop of London, Edmund Grindal:

> Whereas, occasioned by the great want of ministers, we and you both, for tolerable supply thereof, have admitted unto the ministry sundry artificers and others, not traded and brought up in learning, and, as it happened in a multitude, some that were of base occupations: forasmuch as now by experience it is seen that such manner of men, partly by reason of their former profane arts, partly by their light behaviour otherwise and trade of life, are very offensive unto the people, yea, and to the wise of this realm are thought to do a great deal more hurt than good, the Gospel there sustaining slander; these shall be to desire and require you hereafter to be very circumspect in admitting any to the ministry, and only to allow such as, having good testimony of their honest conversation, have been traded and exercised in learning, or at least have spent their time with teaching the children, excluding all others which have been brought up and sustained themselves either by occupation or other kinds of life alienated from learning. This we pray you diligently to look unto, and to observe not only in your own person, but also to signify this our advertisement to other of our brethren, bishops of our province, in as good speed as ye may so that you and they may stay from collating such orders to so unmeet persons, unto such time as in a convocation we may meet together, and have further conference thereof.[57]

[56] Bishop Jewel to Peter Martyr, Salisbury, 6 Nov. 1560, *Zurich Letters,* I (1558—79), No. XXXVIII, p. 92.

A. Tindal Hart, *The Country Clergy in Elizabethan and Stuart Times (1558—1660)* (London: Phoenix House, Ltd., 1958), 11.

[57] Lambeth, 15 Aug. 1560, *Parker's Correspondence,* No. LXXXVI, pp. 120, 121.

The need for parish pastors and deacons had resulted in the ordination of a large number of men in the months after the consecration of Parker as Archbishop. Twenty-two deacons and priests were ordained on 22 Dec. 1559; 10 deacons and readers in January 1560; 14 more received holy orders in February; in March 155 were ordained as deacons or priests on one day by the Bishop of Lincoln at Lambeth. Holy orders, the archbishop said, should be given only to such "as should be found fit for their learning and good conversation, and having sufficient letters testimonial of their virtuous and sober demeanor in the places where they then dwelt, or had dwelt for three years last past, and other things by the law required to be had." [58]

Parker himself felt compelled to issue *An Order for serving of Cures now destitute.* Special care should be exercised by the bishops, he said, to present men to benefices who would actually reside in their cures, who would be willing also to serve neighboring cures in cases of necessity. The principal incumbent was authorized to deputize a deacon "or some honest, sober and grave layman," to act as reader, or lector. He would be permitted to read the appointed order of service, with the litany and the homily. He was not permitted, however, to administer the Sacraments, Baptism and the Holy Supper, or to perform marriages. He was not allowed to "preach or prophesy." Regulations regarding baptisms, catechetical instructions, and Communion attendance were incorporated in the document. Readers were to be appointed only "with the oversight of the bishop, or his chancellor." [59]

Among the Elizabethan clergy were Romanists, Calvinists, Puritans, and a few Lutherans. The persistence of Lutheranism among the clergy has usually been ignored by historians, in spite of the evidence in the original sources. Jewel testified to its existence: "That volatile Ubiquitarian doctrine cannot by any means gain footing among us, though there have not been wanting from the

[58] Strype, *Matthew Parker,* I, 129.

[59] Ibid., I, 130—132; eadem, *Elizabeth,* I, i, 274—277. Hart, op. cit., pp. 27, 28.

first outset those who had the subject much at heart." [60] The fear was expressed that Parliament might order the Religious Settlement in line with the Confession of Augsburg.[61] Hilles was not the only one who was willing to promote, as he wrote, "to the utmost of my power the true religion, of which the chief part is contained in the confession of faith exhibited to the invincible emperor Charles V. at the assembly at Augsburg in 1530." [62] Strype noted:

> As to the Augustan Confession, and how willing many were here to entertain it, Bullinger wrote thus to Utenhovius, a learned man, that had lived in England in king Edward's reign, an assistant to John a Lasco in the German church in London, but now with him in Poland: "I see," said he, "no small disturbances like to rise in England also, if the Augustan Confession be received, which some would have; a thing very unworthy in many regards. This gives vexation to all the purer churches, and would infect them all with its leaven. I pray God restrain men otherwise pious, but sufficiently troublesome to godly men and purer religion." [63]

The supposed Lutheranism of Cecil was not of the strident, confessional sort, [64] and the queen's "diplomatic" Lutheranism was not factious.[65] Lutheranism did not emerge during the Elizabethan Religious Settlement as it did during Henry's break with Rome.

[60] Bishop Jewel to Peter Martyr, Salisbury, 6 Nov. 1560, *Zurich Letters*, I (1558—79), No. XXXVIII, pp. 92 f.

[61] Richard Hilles to Henry Bullinger, London, 28 Feb. 1559, ibid., II (1558—1602), No. VII, p. 17.

[62] Ibid., p. 15.

[63] Strype, *Elizabeth*, I, i, 259. Edward Nares, *Memoirs of the Life and Administration of William Cecil, Lord Burghley* (London: Colburn and Bentley, 1830), II, 51 f.: "Many were for adopting the Augustan Confession of the Lutherans."

[64] Baron Caspar Breuner to the Emperor Ferdinand, London, 6 Aug. 1559, Victor von Klarwill, ed. *Queen Elizabeth and Some Foreigners*, p. 108: "As regards her Majesty's Councillors only her Secretary Cecil is a Lutheran, some others are Zwinglians, some, in my judgment, believe little or nothing."

[65] Count de Feria to Philip II, 29 April 1559, *Span. Cal., Eliz.*, I (1558 to 1567), No. 29, pp. 61, 62: "Subsequently in conversation with me she

The Elizabethan clergy was brought into conformity with the Settlement through visitations. The records of the conformity of the clergy are very incomplete. A Roman Catholic historian stated that 1,804 priests in six of the 18 sees in the province of Canterbury subscribed, and not more than 654 in the four northern dioceses.[66] Different authorities agree, "The question cannot be settled by the data available at present."[67] However: "The one indubitable fact is that the Marian pastorate in overwhelming numbers passed over into the service of the establishment without murmur."[68] The lack of contemporary evidence for the dispossession of a large number of the clergy is a testimony of silence. *The Calendar of Patent Rolls* lists presentations, and in some instances indicates why the positions were void. In 1559, of some 163 names listed for presentations, of which 61 were to rectorages and vicarages before the 1st of June, no reason is given for the vacancy.[69] Forty-six other presentations were made in that year, according to the same record, of which just half were vacated by death; only 15 of the 46 are listed as being due to deprivation.[70] In 1560, of 37 cases

[Elizabeth] said three or four very bad things. One was that she wished the Augustanean confession to be maintained in her realm, whereat I was much surprised and found fault with it all I could, adducing the arguments I thought might dissuade her from it. She then told me it would not be the Augustanean confession, but something else like it, and that she differed very little from us as she believed *that God was in the Sacrament of the Eucharist,* and only dissented from three or four things in the Mass. After this she told me she did not wish to argue about religious matters."

[66] Hughes, *Reformation in England,* III, 39—44.

[67] Black, *Reign of Elizabeth,* p. 17 n.

[68] Ibid., p. 17.
Deprivations, at any rate, were not general. Frere, *Marian Reaction,* pp. 86, 87.
A. G. Dickens, *The Marian Reaction in the Diocese of York,* Part I, The Clergy (St. Anthony's Hall Publications, No. 11; London and York: St. Anthony's Press, 1957), p. 20: "Among the parish clergy singularly few deprivations and resignations seem to have resulted either directly or indirectly from the imposition of the Elizabethan regime."

[69] *Cal. Patent Rolls, Eliz.,* I (1558—60), 122—126.

[70] Ibid., pp. 4, 5, 25, 28, 39, 40, 44, 45, 46, 55, 57, 61, 89, 93, 95, 103, 105, 111.

listed, 14 were due to deprivation.[71] Admittedly the data are too scanty to permit of conclusive generalizing. It may be conjectured, however, that death caused as many vacancies as did deprivations.

Entries in these *Patent Rolls* read, as for instance those for 7 Nov. 1559: "Presentation *(sede vacante)* of William Daye, M. A., to the canonry and prebend of Ampleforth in York Cathedral"; "Presentation *(sede vacante)* of John Watson, clerk, M. A., to the archdeanery of Surrey in Winchester Cathedral, void by the deprivation of Edmund Mervin, clerk" [72] Again, there is the entry for 17 Oct. 1559: "Presentation of John Openshawe, priest, to the rectory of Wrentham, Norwich dioc., void by death." [73] Or again, to cite one more example, on 2 Oct. 1559: "Presentation of Henry Bagwell, clerk, S. T. P., to the rectory of Hatfield alias Hatfield Episcopi, co., Hertford, Lincoln dioc., void by the resignation of John Boxoll, clerk." [74] The details behind entries such as these remain hidden. Why did John Boxoll (whoever he may have been) resign? What did his resignation mean to the people of that parish? Were they happy about it, or sad? What fortitude and conviction did Edmund Mervin, "clerk," show, and why was he deprived of his archdeanery? We simply cannot answer these questions. What were the superior qualifications, if any, and the theological convictions of a William Daye, M. A. (note the degree)? In many parishes there were no changes until death took away the incumbent.

How many conformed because the marriage of the clergy was again permitted? No law of Parliament set aside Queen Mary's repeal [75] of the Edwardian acts which legalized the marriage of priests [76] and legitimatized their children.[77] The royal injunctions

71 Ibid., pp. 252—256.

72 Ibid., p. 4.

73 Ibid., p. 39.

74 Ibid.

75 1 Mary, Statute 2, cap. 2, Gee and Hardy, *Documents,* No. LXXIII, pp. 377—383.

76 2 and 3 Edward VI, cap. 21, ibid., No. LXX, pp. 366—368.

77 5 and 6 Edward VI, cap. 12; cf. ibid., p. 367.

of Queen Elizabeth of 1559, however, provided that a priest or minister of the church "may lawfully, for the avoiding of fornication, have an honest and sober wife." In the days of Edward, however, many ministers had given offense "both in choosing their wives and in indiscreet living with them." Elizabeth, therefore, required that every minister get the consent of the parents or kinsfolk of the prospective bride, the recommendation of two justices of the peace, and the approval of the bishop. The bishops would have to have the approval of the archbishops; deans and heads of colleges needed the approval of a visitation committee.[78] Elizabeth had a strong dislike for married clergy. One bishop wrote: "The Queen's Majesty will wink at it but not stablish it by law, which is nothing else but to bastard our children." [79] Her secretary reported: "Her Majesty continueth very evil affected to the state of matrimony in the clergy." [80] Parker was horrified by her views on the marriage of the clergy; they discomforted and discouraged him.[81] At best the queen tolerated a married clergy. The setting aside of compulsory celibacy made many Protestants in England.

England did not become a wholly Protestant state. It was no longer, it is true, a Roman Catholic country in its outward affiliation. The beliefs of many among the clergy and people were not theologically precise. Perhaps for many the changes in the ceremonies were disturbing, but they got used to them. Gradually some changes in doctrine might be noticed. But the average parishioner knew little of either Roman Catholic or Protestant doctrine. A con-

[78] "The Injunctions of Elizabeth, A. D. 1559," Gee and Hardy, *Documents*, No. LXXVIII, pp. 431, 432, art. xxix.

[79] Dr. Edmund Sandys to Dr. Matthew Parker, London, 30 April 1559, *Parker's Correspondence*, No. XLIX, p. 66.

[80] Sir William Cecil to Archbishop Parker, Smallbridge, 12 Aug. 1561, ibid., No. CVII, p. 148.

[81] Archbishop Parker to Sir William Cecil, 1561, ibid., No. CXIV, pp. 156, 157.

Sir John Neale has set aside the legend of Elizabeth's insult to Parker's wife, *Essays in Elizabethan History,* p. 101.

See Walter H. Frere, *The Marian Reaction in its Relation to the English Clergy* (London: S. P. C. K., 1896), pp. 73—75, for Parker's part in the controversy about the marriage of clergy during Mary's reign.

sciousness of Protestant beliefs was strongest among those of Puritan inclinations. The situation among the clergy, with a side glance at the laity, was summed up in the letter of a contemporary: "The true and sincere doctrine is freely preached throughout England, by those who are known to possess both ability and inclination for this work, by commendatory letters from the queen, or one of the bishops, to authorize the admission of strange preachers into the churches." He did not say, however, how many licensed preachers there were for the eight thousand parishes in England. "No discipline is as yet established by any public authority; but the same order of public prayer, and other ceremonies in the church, which existed under Edward the sixth, is now restored among us by the authority of the queen and parliament; for such is the name of our great council." He wrote about the ornaments and habits of the clergy: ". . . the parish priests in the other churches, retaining the outward habits and inward feeling of popery, so fascinate the ears and eyes of the multitude, that they are unable to believe, but that either the popish doctrine is still retained, or at least that it will shortly be restored." Specifically of the clergy he said: "Many of our parishes have no clergymen, and some dioceses are without a bishop. And out of that very small number who administer the Sacraments throughout this great country, there is hardly one in a hundred who is both able and willing to preach the word of God; but all persons are obliged to read only what is prescribed in the books. Thus indeed is the Lord's harvest very abundant among us, but the labourers are very few." [82]

Always in the church, it seems, faithful laborers and true, are too few.

[82] Thomas Lever to Henry Bullinger, Coventry, 10 July 1560, *Zurich Letters,* I (1558—79), No. XXV, pp. 84, 85.

CHAPTER VI

THE LAITY AND THE ELIZABETHAN
SETTLEMENT

hanges in order and in worship, in doctrine and polity, and among the clergy resulted from the Elizabethan Settlement. There were changes, too, in the church life of the parishes which went beyond the Supremacy Act and the Act of Uniformity. These acts, the essential foundation for the Elizabethan Settlement, were implemented and augmented by proclamations, injunctions, articles of visitations, and the visitations themselves. By these means the broad decisions of Parliament and of the Crown became operative among the laity in the parishes of England.

Within these parishes births and baptisms, banns and marriages, churchings and sick communions and funerals continued. The issues of life and death, of love and devotion, of labor and toil, were close to the people. For some of them the familiar was more meaningful; for others the new was more exciting. Among the parishioners as well as among the clergy there were the radicals, dangerous because of their ignorance, and the ultraconservatives, detrimental because of their stubborn-mindedness. Through it all the church was faced with its age-old tasks of teaching, warning, exhorting, comforting, guiding, forgiving sins and healing consciences, rebuking and condemning those who refused to repent. It reached down into the lives and thoughts of men to a much greater degree in that century than it does in this, more even than among those who today are devoted adherents of the church. The culture of that period was much more ecclesiologically oriented, with strong theological overtones, than is the culture of any country today. True, also the Elizabethans sat down to eat and to drink and to be merry; they, too, were married and given in marriage; they, too, went into other cities to trade and get gain; they, too, wept with the mourners and rejoiced with the joyful. The work of the farmer and the housewife and the miller and the artisan continued with sweat of the brow. So did the ministrations of the church. But, perforce, there were some changes, and changes bring a time of troubles and necessary adjustments. These are little documented, but they are real nevertheless.

Funeral rites, for instance, were changed, yet mourners found in them much that was familiar. Diarists noted funerals, especially of those belonging to the nobility. The obsequies for Frances, Duchess of Suffolk, in Westminster Abbey, on 5 Dec. 1559, are reported to us:

> She was buried in a chapel on the south side of the choir. . . .
> The corpse being brought and set under the hearse, and the mourners placed, the chief at the head, and the rest on each side, Clarenceaux, king of arms, with a loud voice said these words: "Laud and praise be given to Almighty God, that it hath pleased Him to call out of this transitory life unto His eternal glory the most noble and excellent princess Mary, the French queen, daughter of the most illustrious prince king Henry VII." This said, the dean began the service in English for the communion, reciting the ten commandments, and answered by the choir in prick song. After that and other prayers said, the epistle and gospel was read by the two assistants of the dean. After the gospel, the offering began after this manner: first, the mourners that were kneeling stood up: then a cushion was laid and a carpet for the chief mourners to kneel on before the altar: then the two assistants came to the hearse, and took the chief mourner, and led her by the arm, her train being borne and assisted by other mourners following. And after the offering finished, Mr. Jewel began his sermon; which was very much commended by them that heard it.

After sermon, the dean proceeded to the communion; at which were participant, with the said dean, the lady Catherine and the lady Mary, her daughters, among others. When all was over, they came to the Charterhouse in their chariots.[1]

Similar rites on a simpler scale were held in England almost daily. When the bell tolled for the passing of "any Christian body," only one short peal came after the time of his passing, one before the burial, and another short peal after the burial.[2]

For the soul of the departed there was no longer — at least not officially — a place called purgatory. "The doctrine of purgatory taught by the scholastics, and the invocation of the saints, do not have a foundation from the Word of God,"[3] was now official teaching. Private masses and the doctrine "which maintaineth the mass to be a propitiatory sacrifice for the quick and the dead, and a means to deliver souls out of purgatory," were repudiated.[4] These changes in the doctrine and practices of the church meant much in the life of the ordinary parishioner.[5]

In the Eucharist the giving of both the bread and the wine to the communicant was a drastic alteration. This had been the practice during the reign of Edward VI. But the return to the former usage under Queen Mary underscored the change by the Elizabethan Settlement. The external aspects of the Sacrament were of more consequence to many of the laity than the doctrines them-

[1] Strype, *Elizabeth*, I, i, 293. See also pp. 334—336 for a description of the *Celebratio Coenae Domini in funeribus, si amici et vicini defuncti communicare velint.*

[2] Walter H. Frere, ed., *Visitation Articles and Injunctions of the Period of the Reformation*, Alcuin Club Collections, XVI (London: Longmans, Green & Co., 1910), III (1550—75), 62; Strype, *Elizabeth*, I, i, 320 f.

[3] Ibid., I, i, 324.

[4] Ibid., I, i, 327; Charles Hardwick, *A History of the Articles of Religion;* to which is added a series of documents from A. D. 1536 to A. D. 1615 (Cambridge: John Deighton, 1851), Appendix IV: The Eleven Articles, article viii, p. 328.

[5] A. G. Dickens, *The Marian Reaction in the Diocese of York,* Part II, The Laity (St. Anthony Hall Publications, No. 12; London and York: St. Anthony's Press, 1957), 22: "For many pious traditionalists, the cessation of masses for the dead must have occasioned a major spiritual scandal."

selves. The doctrine of transubstantiation, at least in the popular mind, also had called for the veneration of the host. Now the people were taught: "The Sacraments were not ordained of Christ to be gazed upon, or to be carried about; but that we should duly use them." [6]

The external place at which the Lord's Supper was celebrated was important to the laity. The Elizabethan injunctions of 1559 ordered that no altar should be taken down without proper supervision, "wherein no riotous or disordered manner be used." The table, covered, should be set in the place where the altar stood. During the distribution of the Sacrament the table was set forward; after the distribution it was returned to its accustomed place.[7]

The Elizabethan Settlement caused some changes in the practices connected with the Sacrament of Holy Baptism. Exorcism, oil, salt, spittle, the consecrating of the water, "where they pertain not to the substance and necessity of the sacrament," were abolished.[8] Public baptisms were to be ministered in the font, "not in basin, or in any other like thing." [9]

[6] Article XXV of the Thirty-Nine Articles in Hardwick, *A History of the Articles of Religion,* Appendix III, 297.

J. B. Kidd, *The Later Medieval Doctrine of the Eucharistic Sacrifice,* reprint of 1898 ed. (London: SPCK, 1958), for a discussion of Article XXXI.

Dugmore, *The Mass and the English Reformers,* should also be consulted.

[7] "The Injunctions of Elizabeth, A. D. 1559," can be found most conveniently in Gee and Hardy, *Documents,* No. LXXVIII, pp. 417—442. They are found also, e. g., in Frere, *Visitation Articles and Injunctions,* III, 8—29. A 17th-century reprint is in *A Collection of Articles, Injunctions, Canons, Orders, Ordinances, and Constitutions Ecclesiastical; with other Publick Records of the Church of England Chiefly in the Times of K. Edward VI., Q. Elizabeth, K. James, & K. Charles I,* 3d impression with additions (London: Printed for Robert Pawket, 1675), pp. 65—86. Cited as *Collection of Articles.* Subsequent references will be given only to Gee and Hardy, *Documents,* with the pertinent number of article. For the present citation see pp. 439, 440.

[8] Hardwick, *History of the Articles of Religion,* Appendix IV, Eleven Articles, article viii, p. 328; Strype, *Elizabeth,* I, i, 327.

[9] Ibid., I, i, 330.

100

Regarding images, the Elizabethan injunctions repeated only the injunctions of Edward VI. "Besides this, to the intent that all superstition and hypocrisy crept into divers men's hearts may vanish away, they shall not set forth or extol any images, relics, or miracles; they shall teach that all goodness, health, and grace ought to be both asked for and looked for only of God, as of the very Author and Giver of the same, and of none other." [10] Archbishop Matthew Parker drew up a pronouncement against the images which said, "I do utterly disallow the extolling of images, relics, and feigned miracles." To picture God as an old man or the Holy Spirit as a dove, he said, was "vain worshipping of God, devised by man's fantasy" and contrary to Holy Writ. ". . . wandering on pilgrimages, setting up of candles, praying upon beads, and such like superstitions," he held, had no promise of reward in Scripture.[11]

Parker and other bishops petitioned the queen in a most solemn letter regarding images. They expressed themselves humbly but firmly and scholarly. They did not doubt, they stated, that her Majesty would "clearly purge the polluted church, and remove all occasions of evil." They mashaled "certain reasons which move us that we cannot with safe consciences give our assents that the images of Christ, &c. should be placed and erected in churches." These reasons were taken from the Scriptures and "the fathers, councils and histories." They pleaded:

Having thus declared unto your Highness a few causes of many, which do move our consciences in this matter, we beseech your Highness most humbly not to strain us any further; but to consider, that God's word doth threaten terrible judgment unto us, if we, being pastors and ministers in His Church, should assent to the thing which in our learning and conscience we are persuaded doth tend to the confirmation of error, superstition, and idolatry, and finally, to the ruin of souls committed to our charge, for the which we must give an account to the Prince of pastors at the last day.

[10] Gee and Hardy, *Documents,* p. 419, No. II.

[11] Hardwick, *History of the Articles of Religion,* Appendix IV, Eleven Articles, article x, p. 329; Strype, *Elizabeth,* I, i, 328.

They asked that this matter and "suchlike controversies of religion" be referred to a synod of the bishops for discussion and decision.[12] Were the bishops more agitated in this matter than the laity?

Elizabeth had provided in the visitation articles that inquiry should be made "2. *Item,* whether in their churches and chapels all images, shrines, all tables, candlesticks, trinidals, or rolls of wax, pictures, paintings, and all other monuments or feigned and false miracles, pilgrimages, idolatry, and superstition be removed, abolished, and destroyed."[13] At Canterbury Cathedral even certain verses, painted where Thomas à Becket "was wont to be honoured," were ordered destroyed.[14] The objects empirically had been stimuli for some religious acts by the laity. Some welcomed their removal; some opposed it. Processions and rogations were not entirely abolished. The Litany was substituted for all of the processions, except for the beating of the bounds once a year.[15] Days of rogation were still observed.[16]

Within days after the adjournment of Parliament in many churches of London the crucifixes were broken, statues defaced, and altars stripped bare.[17] On St. Bartholomew's Day, 24 Aug. 1559, bonfires were lit from crosses and statues ("Marys and Johns and others images"), copes, vestments, altar cloths, books, and banners.[18]

[12] Archbishop Parker and others to Queen Elizabeth, 1559, *Parker's Correspondence,* No. LXVI, pp. 79—95; Strype, *Elizabeth,* I, i, 331, 332.

[13] "The Royal Articles of Queen Elizabeth, 1559," are found in Frere, *Visitation Articles and Injunctions,* III, 1—7, and in *Collection of Articles,* pp. 175—182. References will be given only to Frere by page and article number. For the present citation see Frere, p. 2, No. 2.

[14] "Parker's Injunctions for Canterbury Cathedral, 1560," in Frere, *Visitation Articles and Injunctions,* III, 79, No. 5.

[15] Gee and Hardy, *Documents,* pp. 425, 426, no. xviii.

[16] Ibid., p. 426 f, no. xix.

[17] Il Schifanoya to Vivaldino, London, 10 May 1559, *Ven. Cal.,* VII, 1558—89, No. 71, p. 84.

[18] *Machyn's Diary,* p. 207; cf. p. 208 for the bonfire at St. Botuelph's on 25 August. Holinshed notes the burnings on 24 August, *Holinshed's Chronicles of England, Scotland, and Ireland* (London, 1808), IV, 185; Strype, *Elizabeth,* I, i, 254 f.

Soon after came a royal proclamation warning against the ruthless destruction of monuments: *A proclamation against breaking or defacing monuments of antiquity; being set up in churches or other public places for memory, and not for superstition.* The statues of famous persons, already defaced, were to be restored. So, too, bells which had been melted for the metal were ordered restored.[19]

Some of the laymen were radical and gave others cause to question the changes in religion. Some of the destruction was antisocial, some anti-Roman and anticlerical.

One item not changed which contributed to anticlericalism was the payment of tithes. The faults of the clergy did not allow for a "restrain or diminution" of the payment of tithes; this would be requiting "one wrong with another."[20] Anticlericalism is indicated in the injunction which said that "many indiscreet persons do at this day uncharitably contemn and abuse priests and ministers of the Church." The ignorance of some of the clergy brought this on in part, in part the persistence of some of them in the doctrines of the Roman Church.[21] The faults of the clergy, however, should not cause the laity to withhold their tithes, the government declared.

These moneys were used in part directly for the benefit of the parish. One fortieth part was distributed to the poor of the parish by the clergy, "lest they be worthily noted of ingratitude."[22] The income from the benefices was used also for the repair of the churches, chapels, and mansions. One fifth of the income was allowed for this purpose.[23]

Churchwardens or "some other honest men of the parish"[24] managed these external affairs of the parish. They were to keep

[19] Ibid., I, i, 279—281. Dated 19 September 1559.

[20] Gee and Hardy, *Documents,* pp. 424, 425, no. xv.

[21] Ibid., pp. 430, 431, no. xxviii.

[22] Ibid., p. 423, no. xi.

[23] Ibid., p. 424, no. xiii. See also Frere, *Visitation Articles and Injunctions,* III, 3, No. 14.

[24] The phrase is taken from Gee and Hardy, *Documents,* p. 423, no. xi. Hart, op. cit., pp. 42, 43.

the church furniture in repair and to administer the parish finances.[25] Specifically, by way of example, the churchwardens were enjoined to provide "a comely and honest pulpit," conveniently located within the church, "for the preaching of God's word."[26] Poor relief was one of the more important aspects of their duties.

The churchwardens provided the poor chest, "a strong chest with a hole in the upper part thereof . . . having three keys." In it the parishioners deposited their alms and oblations. "And also," it was stated, "the money which riseth of fraternities, guilds, and other stocks of the Church . . . and also the rents of lands, the profit of cattle and money given or bequeathed to obits and dirges, or to the finding of torches, lights, tapers, and lamps," should be put into the chest.[27] Church ales, church plays, games, and dances, offerings and gatherings, mortuary fees, were also used to raise money for the church.[28] These gifts and moneys were to be distributed "in the presence of the whole parish, or six of them," to the neediest members. Surplus funds were used for repairing highways or aiding neighboring parishes. Neither the highways nor the poor stood to profit.

Nor was this measure an effective solution to the problem of poor relief. The problem was larger than simple caring for a destitute family or two in a country parish; it involved health services and social welfare in the wider aspects of those terms.[29] The rising cost of living, in spite of the stabilizing of the currency under Elizabeth, and the enclosure movement were only two of the fac-

[25] Sedley L. Ware, "The Elizabethan Parish in Its Ecclesiastical and Financial Aspects," *Johns Hopkins University Studies in Historical and Political Science*, Series XXVI, Nos. 7, 8 (July—August, 1908), pp. 316 to 332. W. P. M. Kennedy, *Elizabethan Episcopal Administration*, Alcuin Club Collection, xxvi (London: A. R. Mowbray & Co., Ltd., 1924), I, cxxx to cxl. Gee and Hardy, *Documents*, p. 435, no. xlvii.

[26] Ibid., pp. 428, 429, no. xxiv.

[27] Gee and Hardy, *Documents*, pp. 429, 430, no. xxv. Frere, *Visitation Articles and Injunctions*, III, 4, no. 27.

[28] Ware, op. cit., *Johns Hopkins Studies in Historical and Political Science*, Series XXVI, Nos. 7, 8 (July—August, 1908), pp. 361—382.

[29] Rowse, *The England of Elizabeth*, pp. 351—355.

tors which complicated this arrangement of caring for the poor. Preachers exhorted their parishioners that

whereas heretofore they have been diligent to bestow much substance, otherwise than God commanded, upon pardons, pilgrimages, trentals, decking of images, offering of candles, giving to friars, and upon other blind devotions, they ought at this time to be much more ready to help the poor and needy, knowing that to relieve the poor is a true worshipping of God, required earnestly upon pain of everlasting damnation, and that also whatever is given for their comfort, is given to Christ Himself, and so is accepted of Him, that He will mercifully reward the same with everlasting life.[30]

Such exhortations might instill piety, but they did not answer all the questions which faced churchwardens in dispensing the contents of the chest for the poor.

The duties of the churchwardens included, furthermore, the enforcement of church attendance. The injunction merely specified that "three or four discreet men, which tender God's glory and His true religion," should be appointed for this purpose.[31] They also were to enforce proper conduct during the church services. *"Item,* that no man shall willingly let [hinder] or disturb the preacher in time of his sermon, or let [hinder] or discourage any curate or minister to sing or say the Divine Service set forth; nor mock or jest at the ministers of such service."[32] Reverence at prayers was specifically enjoined; "lowliness of courtesy and uncovering of heads of menkind" should be made by the worshipers or hearers when the name of Jesus was pronounced in any prayer, Scripture readings, or sermon.[33] Again, it was ordered: *"Item,* that

[30] Gee and Hardy, *Documents,* pp. 429, 430, no. xxv.

[31] Ibid., p. 434, no. xlvi; J. S. Purvis, ed. *Tudor Parish Documents of the Diocese of York* (Cambridge: The University Press, 1948), pp. 74 to 81.

[32] Gee and Hardy, *Documents,* p. 433, no. xxxvi; Frere, *Visitation Articles and Injunctions,* III, 5, no. 32; Purvis, *Tudor Parish Documents,* pp. 82—95.

[33] Gee and Hardy, *Documents,* pp. 437, 438, no. lii.

no man, woman, or child shall be otherwise occupied in the time of the service than in quiet attendance to hear, mark and understand that is read, preached and ministered." [34] In the larger churches, such as the cathedral church of York, walking around during the sermon, brawling, and disorders were not unknown.[35]

A frequent cause of disputes in the parish churches was the growing custom of establishing family pews or stalls. This custom was accelerated during the reign of Edward VI, both by religious and by social changes. At the end of the century some property holders and some officials, among them especially the churchwardens, claimed the right to erect pews or stalls in the parish church for themselves and their families.[36]

Within the Elizabethan parish the schoolmaster and the parish clerk were important. The parish clerk was required to read the Epistle and the psalms in the divine services, to make the responses to the suffrages, to keep the church and its appointments clean, "and also that he endeavor himself to teach the young children to read, if he be able to do so." [37]

Parish clerks and teachers alike needed the consent of the Ordinary to perform such duties. The schoolmaster, or teacher, was to be "found meet as well for his learning and dexterity in teaching, as for sober and honest conversation, and also for right understanding of God's true religion." [38] They were to incite the children "to the love and due reverence of God's true religion now truly set forth by public authority." [39] They should require their pupils to learn "such sentences of Scripture as shall be most expedient to

[34] Ibid., p. 433, no. xxxviii.

[35] Purvis, *Tudor Parish Documents*, p. 83.

[36] Ibid., pp. 87—91. Hart, op. cit., p. 42.

[37] Purvis, *Tudor Parish Documents*, pp. 189, 190. See also Kennedy, *Eliz. Episc. Adm.*, I, cxliii, cxliv.

[38] Gee and Hardy, *Documents*, pp. 433, 434, no. xl. See also Kennedy, *Eliz. Episc. Adm.*, I, cxl—cxlii.

[39] Gee and Hardy, *Documents*, p. 431, no. xli.

106

induce them to all godliness."[40] The schoolmasters used the grammar text of Henry VIII "and none other."[41]

The teaching of the catechism, according to the rubric of the Elizabethan Prayer Book,[42] was the duty of "every parson, vicar, and curate." On holy days and on every other Sunday they were to devote a half hour "at the least" before vespers in the instruction of all the youths of the parish in the Decalog, the Creed, and the Lord's Prayer.[43] Grindal as Archbishop of York directed the clergy: "*Item,* you shall every Sunday and holy-day openly in your church or chapel call for, hear, and instruct the children and servants both menkind and womenkind that be of convenient age within your parish . . . before evening prayer in the ten commandments, the articles of the belief, and the Lord's prayer in English, and diligently examine and teach them the catechism set forth in the Book of Common Prayer."[44] Parents, too, were to teach their children these three chief parts of the Christian faith.[45] The laity was to be an indoctrinated laity.

For the advancement of Protestantism the royal injunctions ordered a Bible set up in every parish church together with the *Paraphrases of Erasmus.* The reading of the Scriptures was encouraged because they are "the very lively Word of God."[46] No one was to reason or dispute "rashly and contentiously" about the Holy Scriptures, nor maintain any false doctrine or error.[47] The licensing of printers was ordered by the royal injunction, partly because of the "heretical, seditious, and unseemly" literature being printed.[48] The visitation articles directed inquiry about the reading of Scrip-

[40] Ibid., no. xlii.

[41] Ibid., p. 433, no. xxxix; Frere, *Visitation Articles and Injunctions,* III, p. 4, no. 30

[42] *Liturgical Services,* p. 210. See Chap. 4. fn. 1.

[43] Gee and Hardy, *Documents,* p. 434, no. xliv.

[44] Purvis, *Tudor Parish Documents,* p. 129.

[45] Gee and Hardy, *Documents,* p. 420, no. v.

[46] Ibid., p. 421, no. vi.

[47] Ibid., p. 433, no. xxxvii.

[48] Ibid., pp. 436, 437, no. li.

ture[49] as well as the making and buying and selling of unlawful books.[50]

The injunctions and visitation articles give a partial picture of activities and conditions within the parishes of England. In spite of irregularities, piety and morality and genuine religion were found among the common people, the laity. Articles which directed that inquiry should be made about common drunkards, swearers, blasphemers, adulterers, fornicators, incestuous persons, or bawds, brawlers, slanderers, chiders, scolders, and sowers of discord[51] reckoned with the weaknesses of human nature without indicting a whole parish or a people. Some alehouses remained open during the time of Common Prayer,[52] and some of the clergy were "common haunters and resorters to taverns or alehouses, giving themselves to drinking, rioting and playing at unlawful games."[53]

The enforcement of injunctions and the Parliamentary enactments devolved in part on the churchwardens and the parish clergy. The diocesan officials also had jurisdiction. Besides the Court of the Bishop and the Archdeacon's Court, there were the courts of the Archbishop, the Consistory Court, the Court of Audience, the Court of Peculiars, and the Prerogative Court. The High Court of Delegates and the Court of High Commission ranked above the courts of the Archbishop.[54]

The visitations, however, were the chief means by which the Religious Settlement was enforced in England. The visitors were sent out by royal command to each of the parishes in a given district. The cathedral houses and chapter houses were visited.

[49] Frere, *Visitation Articles and Injunctions*, III, 2, no. 6.

[50] Ibid., III, 7, no. 52; cf. Purvis, *Tudor Parish Documents*, pp. 148 to 150.

[51] Frere, *Visitation Articles and Injunctions*, III, 5, nos. 34, 35, 36.

[52] Ibid., III, 5, no. 40.

[53] Ibid., III, 2, no. 7.

[54] J. R. Tanner, ed. *Tudor Constitutional Documents, A. D., 1485 to 1603, with an Historical Commentary* (Cambridge: The University Press, 1922), pp. 358—362. See also Sir Maurice Powicke, *The Reformation in England,* 4th impression (London: Oxford University Press, 1953), pp. 119 to 124.

Inquiry was made concerning fifty-six points. Laymen and clergy alike served on these visitation commissions.[55] One report read:

We found every where the people sufficiently well disposed towards religion, and even in those quarters where we expected most difficulty. It is however hardly credible what a harvest, or rather what a wilderness of superstition had sprung up in the darkness of the Marian times. We found in all places votive relics of saints, nails with which the infatuated people dreamed that Christ had been pierced, and I know not what small fragments of the sacred cross. The number of witches and sorceresses had every where become enormous. The cathedral churches were nothing else but dens of thieves, or worse, if any thing worse or more foul can be mentioned. If inveterate obstinacy was found any where, it was altogether among the priests, those especially who had once been on our side. They are now throwing all things into confusion, in order, I suppose, that they may not seem to have changed their opinions without due consideration. But let them make what disturbance they please; we have in the mean time disturbed them from their rank and office.[56]

The injunctions administered for some of the cathedrals bear out, at least in part, these observations. At Wells Cathedral, the injunctions say, "it doth appear small devotion and much negligence to be in the dignities and canons and residentiaries of this church both in ministering and receiving of the Communion."[57] Sundry members, they found, "seek rather their own profits than the good orders in the said foundation comprehended."[58] The royal injunctions for Worcester Cathedral, like those for the Exeter Cathedral, warned against giving occasion for suspicions of immorality.[59] In other cases the answers returned for the royal visitation indicate

[55] Strype, *Elizabeth*, I, i, 242—256.

[56] John Jewel to Peter Martyr, London, 2 Nov. 1559, *Zurich Letters*, I (1558—79), No. XIX, pp. 44, 45.

[57] "Royal Injunctions for Wells Cathedral, 1559," Frere, *Visitation Articles and Injunctions*, III, 37, no. 13.

[58] Ibid., no. 14.

[59] "Royal Injunctions for Worcester Cathedral, 1559," ibid., III, 45, no. 2; "Royal Injunctions for Exeter Cathedral, 1559," ibid., III, 41, no. 26.

a quite satisfactory state of affairs,[60] evidenced by a continued care for the good order of the churches.[61]

The episcopal visitations, which replaced the royal visitation of 1559, were within the framework of the royal injunctions of that year; often the very words of the royal injunctions were repeated in the episcopal visitation articles and injunctions.[62] Although the archbishops and bishops were civil servants, they were, unlike medieval prelates, used as ecclesiastical officials. The disorderly affairs of the dioceses could be corrected, and the bishops were able to improve the conditions among the parish clergy.[63] If the adage "Like priest, like people" is true, this would mean that the influence of the church would pervade the people to a greater degree and a strengthening of piety and morality and genuine religion among the common parishioners, the laity, would result.

This piety of the laity was not without consequence for nationalism. The majesty of the ruler was exalted by the Act of Supremacy, and her designation as "Supreme Governess" of the church meant additional power and prestige for the queen. Although laymen did not have to take the oath acknowledging the queen's supremacy, "the chief government of all estates, ecclesiastical and civil, in all causes within this dominion" [64] was recognized as

[60] E. g., "Royal Visitation of Canterbury Cathedral, 1559," ibid., III, 49—53.

[61] "Parker's Injunctions for Canterbury Cathedral, 1560," ibid., III, 78—86; see also pp. 140—142 for "Archbishop Parker's Diocesan Articles, 1563."
Parker's articles and injunctions are merely an example of other diocesan articles and injunctions after 1559. Jewel, Grindal, Horne, Guest, Bentham, Parkhurst, Cox, Sandys, among others, issued such articles. Ibid., III, 94—386, passim. See also Kennedy, *Eliz. Episc. Adm.*, II (Visitation Articles and Injunctions, 1575—82); III (Visitation Articles and Injunctions, 1583—1603).

[62] E. T. Davis, *Episcopacy and the Royal Supremacy in the Church of England in the XVI Century* (Oxford: Basil Blackwell, 1950), 79.

[63] Rowse, *The England of Elizabeth*, p. 391.

[64] Thomas Rogers, *The Catholic Doctrine of the Church of England: An Exposition of the Thirty-Nine Articles*, edited for the Parker Society by J. J. S. Perome (Cambridge: The University Press, 1854), p. 335. Cited as Rogers, *Thirty-Nine Articles*.

110

belonging to the monarch. This was not simply the substitution of one head for another. The bishop of Rome was a foreigner; the ruler of England was a native. The bishop of Rome could enforce his wishes only indirectly, using ecclesiastical sanctions; the ruler of England could bring about compliance directly, by force if need be, using both civil and ecclesiastical sanctions. However, the laity did not make nationalism a religion or the queen a goddess. Protestantism contributed to nationalism, and civic morality furthered patriotism. Fearsome as civic sanctions might be, the ecclesiastical sanctions were the more fearful.

Excommunication, both greater and lesser excommunication, entailed social and civic disabilities as well as severe spiritual ones.[65] It was applied to those who perverted "the sound doctrine of the truth" and to those "defiled with notorious wickedness." [66] Its purpose was to restore the sinner to the truth or to virtuous living by true repentance. Excommunication, too, was to act as a deterrent to sin for others, "that good and virtuous persons may not be infected through the continual or much familiarity of the wicked," [67] since avoiding an excommunicated person meant that he was "not to be eaten withal, not to be companied withal, not to be received into the house." [68] This sanction was not applied often; the threat of its use in most instances brought about outward compliance, at least. Excommunication in a state-governed church involved action also by civil authorities. It was a civil offense to remain in a state of excommunication. Notorious sinners were not admitted to Holy Communion.[69] The excommunicated were barred from church if they tried to attend; they were liable to fines if they failed to attend.

Regular church attendance was made compulsory by the Act of Uniformity. For their instruction, edification, comfort, and improvement in Christian living, the laity were obliged to hear at least

[65] Kennedy, *Eliz. Episc. Adm.,* I, cxxv, cxxvi.

[66] Rogers, *Thirty-Nine Articles,* p. 308.

[67] Ibid., p. 312.

[68] Ibid., p. 308.

[69] Gee and Hardy, *Documents,* pp. 427, 428, no. xxi.

one sermon a month wherein "purely and sincerely" they were exhorted "to the works of faith, as mercy and charity, specially prescribed and commanded in Scripture." [70]

The lives of the laity centered in the church. The parish register of all weddings, baptisms, and burials [71] is symbolical of the central position of the church in the lives of the common people of Elizabethan England.

[70] Ibid., p. 419, no. iiii; cf. p. 420, no. iv, re reading of the *Homilies*.

[71] Ibid., pp. 422, 423, no. x. Frere, *Visitation Articles and Injunctions*, III, 2, no. 10.

CHAPTER VII

THE OLD RELIGION AND THE
ELIZABETHAN SETTLEMENT

When Queen Mary was buried on 14 Dec. 1558 the hopes of many of the adherents of the Old Religion were buried with her. Death robbed the Romanists of other leaders. Reginald Cardinal Pole, archbishop of Canterbury, had died on the day of Mary's death. Maurice Griffin, bishop of Rochester and parson of St. Magnus on Londonbridge, passed away three days later. Christopherson, bishop of Chichester, died in December. Ten of the twenty-six bishoprics were vacant at the end of January 1559.

The indiscreet remarks of the bishop of Winchester, in his funeral sermon for Queen Mary, difficult to reconstruct at this time, had caused his house arrest. Other members of the clergy, fearing an alteration in religion, preached "lewdly," to use the phraseology of that day, that is, objectionably. Some priests were arrested for their preaching, for they (as did some Protestants) continued to preach even after the queen's proclamation of 27 December which forbade preaching except by special license. Among the clergy, too, there were those who made snide references to the circumstances of Elizabeth's birth. However, "An Act for the explanation of the statute of seditious words and rumours," was directed only against the Roman Catholics. It re-enacted a law from the previous

113

reign which made slander and malicious words a cause for pillorying, or loss of land, or a large fine.[1]

The refusal of almost all the bishops to participate in the queen's coronation alarmed some of Elizabeth's subjects. It was an indication of the opposition which she would receive in the House of Lords to any program of religious alteration. At the beginning of the parliamentary session the clergy met in convocation to deliberate on these changes; they were largely concerned with the question of how the Old Religion might be retained. They framed a protest against doctrinal innovations, asking for the preservation of the doctrine "handed down from the Apostles even to ourselves." The idea that any government had the right to define matters of faith and doctrine or matters dealing with the sacraments and with church discipline was entirely repugnant to them. These matters belonged to the clergy. They formulated five propositions on the chief points of doctrine they held were in need of defense. They said:

We affirm, and, so God help us in the day of judgment, we assert:

I. That in the sacrament of the altar, by virtue of the words of Christ, duly spoken by the priest, is present *realiter,* under the kinds of bread and wine, the natural body of Christ, conceived of the virgin Mary, and also his natural blood.

II. That after the consecration there remains not the substance of bread and wine, nor any other substance but the substance of God and man.

III. That in the mass is offered the true body of Christ, and his true blood, a propitiatory sacrifice for the living and the dead.

IV. That to Peter the apostle, and his lawful successors in the apostolic see, as Christ's vicars, is given the supreme power of feeding and ruling the church of Christ militant, and confirming their brethren.

V. That the authority of handling and defining concerning the things belonging to faith, sacraments, and discipline ecclesiastical, hath hitherto ever belonged, and ought to belong only to the

[1] *L. J.,* I, 579. See Chap. V, fn. 5.

pastors of the church; whom the Holy Ghost for this purpose hath set in the church; and not to laymen.

We, the aforesaid lower clergy, for the reasons we have mentioned, by the tenor of these presents, set forth to Your Paternities this our assertion and our affirmation and our faith.[2]

The petition did not affect the course of the legislation, since the Marian bishops remained a minority in Parliament throughout the session. They were not deprived of the sees until proper legislation had been passed; their presence in Parliament furnished opposition, but it could not prevent the Elizabethan Settlement.[3] Nevertheless, their opposition must be noted. One of the reformers complained: "The bishops are a great hindrance to us; for being, as you know, among the nobility and leading men in the upper house, and having none there on our side to expose their artifices and confute their falsehoods, they reign as sole monarchs in the midst of ignorant and weak men, and easily overreach our little party either by their numbers or their reputation for learning." [4]

In the course of the debates in the House of Lords two outstanding speeches were delivered. The first was by Nicholas Heath, archbishop of York, in connection with the Bill of Supremacy. To him a break with Rome would be a severance with the catholic or the universal church, and no longer would it be possible to say, "I believe in the holy catholic church." Those who separate themselves from Rome also repudiate the general councils, the councils of Nicaea, Constantinople, Ephesus, and Chalcedon. Besides that, all Christian princes, "whether they be protestant or catholic," have refrained from taking the title of supremacy, except Henry VIII. The "unity of Christ's church" would be shattered by the action of Parliament in passing the Act of Supremacy. "Therefore by leaping out of Peter's ship, we must needs be overwhelmed with

[2] Strype, *Elizabeth,* I, i, 81; Hughes, *Reformation in England,* III, 22, 23.

[3] D'Ewes remarked from time to time about Elizabeth's moderation in contrast to the boldness and perverseness of the bishops. See, e. g., *Journals,* pp. 50, 51, 23, 24, 26.

[4] John Jewel to Peter Martyr, London, 20 March 1559, *Zurich Letters,* I (1558—79), No. 5, p. 10.

the waters of schism, sects, and divisions," he said. He cited the example of the Germanys as proof. Moreover, the granting of the supremacy to the queen is the granting of a spiritual supremacy. This carries with it the right to loose and to bind, to teach, to confirm (strengthen) the brethren, and to excommunicate. Parliament, he pointed out, does not have the authority to say to anyone, "I give unto you the keys of the kingdom of heaven." It does not have the authority to commission anyone to teach in the church. No woman, he stated, has the right to preach or administer the sacraments, or to excommunicate. "But a woman, in the decrees of Christ's church, is not called to be an apostle, nor evangelist, nor to be a shepherd, neither a doctor or preacher. Therefore, she cannot be supreme head of Christ's militant church, nor yet any part thereof." [5]

The second speech was by Cuthbert Scot, bishop of Chester. He hesitated to speak against the Bill of Supremacy, he said, because the queeen was involved. He acknowledged obedience to her, "not only for wrath and displeasure's sake, but for conscience' sake, and that by the Scriptures of God." Deference, too, to other members of the House of Lords, made him reluctant to speak. He, too, pleaded for unity. Unity is a guiding principle in the civil order, and unity is maintained in the ecclesiastical order "in Christ's church." Christ, he argued, has "appointed one governor to rule and lead them [His people] outwardly." This governor is not a temporal prince. God gave Peter the keys of the kingdom of heaven.

Scot examined the objections to the pope's supremacy, for instance, the reputation for wicked and evil lives which some of the popes of Rome acquired. "A man is a man," he retorted, none is sinless. He argued that St. Augustine acknowledged "the supremacy of St. Peter and his successors." The Greek Church, according to him, acknowledged Rome's supremacy for eight hundred years. Those countries that have renounced the pope's authority, as Germany, Denmark, and Poland, have suffered calamities since their break with the Church of Rome. Neither in Lutheran Denmark

[5] Strype, *Elizabeth,* I, ii, 399—407, Appendix No. VI.

nor in Germany did anyone take it upon himself to be called *supreme head of the church*. The reference to an alleged provincial council of clergy in England which repudiated the authority of the Roman bishop was put aside by him. No temporal prince can appoint anyone as head or governor of the church, the office which belongs to Peter and his successors, he argued.

Scot then argued against the reformers.

Now if a man should ask of these men in this realm, which dissent from the [Roman] Catholic Church, not only in this point of the supremacy, but also in diverse of the chief mysteries of our faith, of whom they learned this doctrine which they hold and teach, they must needs answer, that they learned it of the Germanies. Then we may demand of them again, of whom the Germanies did learn it? Whereunto they must answer, that they learned it of Luther. Well, then of whom did Luther learn it? Whereunto he shall answer himself in his book that he wrote *De Missa angulari, seu privata:* where he saith, that such things as he teacheth against the Mass, and the blessed Sacrament of the Altar, he learned of Satan, the Devil. At whose hands it is like he did also receive the rest of his doctrine. Then here be two points diligently to be noted. First, that this doctrine is not yet fifty years old; for no man taught it before Luther. And secondly, that Luther doth confess and acknowledge the Devil to be his schoolmaster in diverse points of his doctrine.

After divesting himself of this observation, he remarked:

So that now we may be bold to stand in our doctrine and religion against our adversaries, saying that theirs is not yet fifty years old, and ours above fifteen hundred years old. They have for authority and commendation of their religion Luther and his schoolmaster before mentioned; we have for ours St. Peter and his master Christ.[6]

[6] Ibid., I, ii, 408—423, Appendix No. VII. Hughes, *Reformation in England*, III, 23, n. 2, called attention to the fact that the Catholic Truth Society of London recently reprinted the speeches of Heath and Scot under the title *The New Religion*.

These speeches dealt with the issue of the supremacy. Their arguments became the stock in trade of the Old Religionists in England against the Elizabethan Settlement. Additional arguments in favor of the pope and continued union with the Roman Church were supplied in a short discourse by an unknown author. He used the words of the Creed as his theme.

The church is one, he pointed out. "But if you say, that it is *one* through this, that it hath one faith, then may I well reply, that one faith is kept nowhere, without there be one head. Otherwise, why be there Lutherans, Zwinglians, Pacemontaines? Which all do challenge the Scripture, and none of them acknowledge one head, whereby they should be one. No, the very Lutherans be not one, nor in one faith, but so long as they obey their master Luther."

That church is apostolic which can trace its descent from the apostles, he continued. He referred to the apostolic succession of the bishops. Then he asked: Which church is holy? "Is it not the church commonly called *popish?* Hath it not flourished this *{sic}* fifteen hundred years? Contrariwise the Lutheran and the Zwinglian churches were not, by their own confession, in any place or number these seven hundred years."

The word "catholic," he said next, means universal. In time and place the Roman Church is universal. Which church, he asked, is more universal, that "named of Christ" or that "named of Luther and Zwinglius. . . . Are there not more papists in these days, as they term them, than Lutherans?" There was no bishop "in the whole pedigree of their opinions before them." Their church, he concluded, is neither one, nor holy, nor catholic, nor apostolic; the church they call "papistical . . . that church, I say, is only the true church." [7]

In the House of Lords the adherents of the Old Religion also debated the Act of Uniformity. Fecknam, abbot of Westminster, and again, Scot, bishop of Chester, spoke against the bill. In these two orations are given the arguments which would be repeatedly voiced against the change.

[7] Strype, *Elizabeth,* I, ii, 451—456, Appendix No. XI.

118

Fecknam argued that the Old Religion is the true religion and that the religion to be established by act of Parliament is counterfeit. The Old Religion is steadfast and consistent; the new religion is not. As proof of the inconsistency of the new religion he cited the German writers, "the chief schoolmasters and instructors of our countrymen in all these novelties." He pointed to the disagreement of Martin Luther and Philip Melanchthon with the teachings of Carlstadt; Zwingli disagreed with Luther. Peter Martyr did not agree with the doctrines of Luther or Zwingli about the Lord's Supper. He showed that Cranmer in his catechism and Ridley at Paul's Cross had taught the Real Presence; later they denied this doctrine. He said, too, that now, at the beginning of Elizabeth's reign, obedience, humility, meekness, and chastity have been displaced by disobedience, pride, contempt, and fleshly and carnal liberty. Such are the fruits of the new religion, he would have his hearers believe.[8]

Scot, the bishop of Chester, also spoke against the Bill of Uniformity. He found that the disunity of the church took away charity. Hope is destroyed. The certainty of faith would hang upon an act of Parliament, "a weak staff to lean unto." Faith and religion ought not to be subject to the vagaries of a body of lay Lords and Commoners; the bill deals with a matter of life and death, not to be passed over lightly. He examined the Order for the Administration of the Holy Sacrament. It takes away the sacrifice. No sacrifice, no priesthood; no priesthood, no religion; no religion, no God. So he argued. There is no body and blood of Christ present in this Sacrament, for there is no consecration at all, and there can be no worship of Christ. He cited the Lutherans to show that they believe the Real Presence and referred to the Zwinglians, who taunted the Lutherans that therefore they ought to worship the host. He warned the Lords about the great danger and peril to which they are exposing themselves if they made themselves judges in this matter. Ancient heresies were reviewed to show that in times past other temporal rulers had refused to legislate regarding spiritual matters. Theodosius and Valentine

[8] Ibid., I, ii, 431—438, Appendix No. IX.

found it unlawful to determine matters of doctrine because they were laymen. "But to conclude; and if these emperors had not to do with such matters, how should your lordships have to do with all?" [9]

Such arguments did not prevent the passage of the bill, but they provided the Romanists with a pattern of objections which they used for years against the Elizabethan Settlement.

The objection of the bishops voiced at the Westminster Disputation on the 31st of March should also be noted. They said: "We are of the catholic church, and abide therein, and stand in the possession of the truth." The Protestants protested: "We . . . are of the true Catholic church, and maintain the verity thereof." The bishops wanted to determine to which church the Protestants belonged, "for there are many churches in Germany." [10] The Westminster Disputation, however, came to an abrupt and inglorious end and added nothing to the store of Roman Catholic argumentative weapons.

The debate between Romanists and Protestants continued outside Parliament. The Great Controversy, as it was called, reached its crest between 1562 and 1567; it produced works belonging to the glory of English literature. Thomas Harding and John Jewel were the leaders on the Roman Catholic and the Protestant side respectively.

Bishop John Jewel had delivered a sermon at St. Paul's Cross on 26 Nov. 1559 "before a very great confluence of auditors." [11] In this sermon he issued a challenge to the clergy of the Old Reli-

[9] Ibid., I, ii, 438—450, Appendix No. X.

[10] The quotations are from Foxe, *Acts and Monuments,* ed. Cattley, VIII, 690, 691. Henry N. Birt, *The Elizabethan Religious Settlement* (London: George Bell and Sons, 1907), pp. 98—119, presented the best account from the Roman Catholic viewpoint.

The House of Commons recessed on 3 April to hear the disputation, so the clerk recorded it, between the bishops and Mr. Horne, Mr. Cocks [Cox], "and other *Englishmen,* that came from *Geneva." C. J.,* I, 59.

D'Ewes wrote, *Journals,* p. 53: "Her Majesties godly desire to abolish superstition, and to preserve Unity and Truth in the Church, doth fully appear, by the appointment and permission of this disputation . . ."

[11] Strype, *Elizabeth,* I, i, 200.

gion to show out of Scriptures, the church fathers, or the example of the primitive church that private masses, Communion under one kind, worship in a "strange tongue," or the authority of the bishop of Rome were allowed. He offered to subscribe to any of the Roman doctrines if they be so established.[12] The sermon was repeated on 17 March 1560 and again on 31 March 1560. Dr. Cole entered the lists against Jewel; the main attack, however, came from Thomas Harding, whose *An Answere to Maister Iuelles Chalenge* discussed each of Jewel's twenty-seven articles.[13] Jewel replied with his *Apologia ecclesiae anglicanae* (1562) or, as translated into English by Lady Bacon, *An Apologie or answere in defence of the Churche of Englande with a briefe and plaine declaratione of the true Religion professed and vsed in the same* (1564).[14] Harding's *A Confutation of a Booke intituled An Apologie of the Church of England* (1565) [15] received in answer Jewel's lengthy treatise, *A Defence of the Apologie of the Churche of England Conteining an Answer to a certaine Booke lately set forth by M. Harding, and entituled, A Confutation of &c.* (1567).[16]

Harding regarded the Church of England as heretical; "they be not in nor of the church." [17] The Roman Church, he said, has the truth, not Hus, Wyclif, and other heretics.[18] Division and schism followed on Luther's preaching.[19] ". . . it [your religion] began,

[12] Ibid., I, i, 300, 301; A. C. Southern, *Elizabethan Recusant Prose,* 1559—82 (London and Glasgow: Sands & Co., Ltd., [1950]), 60.

[13] *S. T. C.* 12758 (See Chap. 1, fn. 16); Southern, *Eliz. Recusant Prose,* p. 62 (16).

[14] *The Works of John Jewel,* edited for the Parker Society by John Ayre (Cambridge: The University Press, 1848), III, 5—47 for the Latin, 52—108 for the English; Southern, *Eliz. Recusant Prose,* p. 16 (12), (13).

[15] *S. T. C.* 12762; Southern, *Eliz. Recusant Prose,* p. 63 (27).

[16] *Jewel's Works,* III, 150—626; Southern, *Eliz. Recusant Prose,* p. 65 (58); *S. T. C.* 14600.

[17] *Jewel's Works,* III, 151. Harding's text has been followed as given by Jewel, because it was most readily at hand in that form.

[18] Ibid., III, 161; cf. pp. 184 ff., 187 f., 212.

[19] Ibid., III, 174, 181, 253, 601.

121

not at Jerusalem, but at Wittenberg." [20] He referred to the spread of Roman Catholicism in the New World and in the Far East to refute the boast that many cities and kings have come over to the Protestants.[21] He also asked: "When ye preach only faith, not to remove the merits of works before baptism, as St. Paul meant it, but also after baptism; when ye take away the sacrament of confession and absolution, give ye not the bridle to all naughtiness?" [22] But his chief concern was to brand his opponents as heretics.

Alongside the Scriptures, Harding used "the authority of the holy fathers, of ancient traditions, and of the universal church." [23] The church is the interpreter of Scripture.[24] This church is the catholic, or universal, church,[25] of which the pope, as the successor of Peter, is the head.[26]

Harding denied that the English bishops were in the apostolic succession. He asked: "How many bishops can you reckon, whom in the church of Salisbury you have succeeded as well in doctrine as in outward sitting in that chair?" [27] The office of preaching and of absolution, he also maintained, are not to be confused.[28] There are two keys, the key of order and the key of jurisdiction; the key

[20] Ibid., III, 193.

[21] Ibid., III, 193.

[22] Ibid., III, 169

[23] Ibid., III, 231—233.

[24] Ibid., III, 240, 241.

[25] Ibid., III, 265—267, 310.

[26] Ibid., III, 286.

[27] Ibid., III, 320; cf. pp. 320—322. "But order and consecration you have not," p. 322.

Leo XIII on 13 Sept. 1896, in the encyclical *Apostolicae curae,* ruled: ". . . So it came about, since the sacrament of ordination and the true Christian priesthood has been utterly cast out of the Anglican rite, and thus in the consecration of bishops of the said rite no priesthood is conferred, so no episcopacy can be truly or rightly conferred. . . ." Henry Bettenson, ed. *Documents of the Christian Church,* Galaxy ed. (New York and London: Oxford University Press, 1947), pp. 384, 385.

[28] *Jewel's Works,* III, 354—356, 361.

of knowledge (or the key of discretion) and the key of power are subdivisions of these.[29] The clergy, exercising these powers, are to be unmarried.[30]

Turning from the doctrine of the church and the ministry, Harding took up the doctrine concerning the Scriptures, particularly the question of the canon.[31] He next turned to the question of the sacraments, defending the Roman doctrine of the seven sacraments, transubstantiation, the Mass, and Communion under one kind, and attacking the doctrine of the Church of England with its "abasement of our Lord's Supper."[32] Purgatory,[33] ceremonies,[34] the mediation of saints,[35] and the efficacy of good works for salvation[36] are all defended by him.

Harding's arguments repeated much that had already been said by previous defenders of the Roman faith; the same arguments would be used time and again by others. Heresy! heresy! heresy! was the warning cry which the apologetes of the Old Religion raised. Nicholas Heath used that word to Elizabeth when she stood in the presence of the bishops, asking them to take the oath of supremacy. Mary, he said, had restored allegiance to the see of Peter and had promised "to depress heresies and all heretical books." Under the same kind of covenant the pope would welcome Elizabeth "after so long a heresy increasing within this isle."[37]

Heresy was the charge made by the pope in his attempt to order the relations between the Roman Catholics of England and the queen. Giovanni Piero Caraffa, Paul IV, was the bishop of Rome

[29] Ibid., III, 363, 378, 379, 381; cf. pp. 366—369.

[30] Ibid., III, 386, 387, 411, 412.

[31] Ibid., III, 429—431

[32] Ibid., III, 442—444, 449, 450, 455—457, 460, 461, 465, 466, 472, 473, 484, 485, 488—491, 506, 523—526, 550—552.

[33] Ibid., III, 559, 563—565.

[34] Ibid., III, 569.

[35] Ibid., III, 572 f.

[36] Ibid., III, 582 f.

[37] Strype, *Elizabeth,* I, i, 207.

at the time of Elizabeth's accession. Edward Crane was the official ambassador of the realm to the pope. Elizabeth did not choose to notify the pope of her accession.[38] Paul IV, under the prompting of Philip II of Spain, was ready to follow a moderate course, although his personal convictions seem to have been that Elizabeth ought to be excommunicated. Before dealing with Elizabeth directly, however, he issued the bull *Cum ex apostolatus officio* (15 Feb. 1559). Heresy and friendship with heretics on the part of rulers and princes and nobles was declared a bar to office; the pope had been given authority, the bull declared, over nations and people.[39] Pius V repeated the same claims in his bull *Regnans in excelsis* (25 Feb. 1570), in which he excommunicated and deposed Elizabeth of England by name because of her heresy.[40]

Paul IV had died on 18 Aug. 1559; his successor was Pius IV. Pius IV was of a more conciliatory nature than Paul IV had been; he would make several attempts to win Elizabeth back to the Roman Church. For Elizabeth the relations with the papacy were part of the diplomatic game, which involved particularly Philip II. The mission of Parpaglia as papal nuncio to Elizabeth, although he was never permitted to enter England, was so regarded.[41]

[38] F. W. Maitland, "The Anglican Settlement and the Scottish Reformation," ch. xvi in *The Cambridge Modern History* (New York: The Macmillan Co., 1934), II, 564; A. O. Meyer, *England and the Catholic Church under Elizabeth*, p. 20; John H. Pollen, *The English Catholics in the Reign of Queen Elizabeth*, a study of their politics, civil life, and government, 1558—80, from the fall of the Old Religion to the advent of the Counter Reformation (London: Longmans, Green & Co., 1920), p. 59.

[39] Carl Mirbt, ed. *Quellen zur Geschichte des Papsttums und des Römischen Katholizismus*, 4th ed. (Tuebingen: Verlag von J. C. B. Mohr [Paul Siebeck], 1924). No. 440, pp. 288, 289; Sidney Z. Ehler and John B. Morrall, eds. *Church and State Through the Centuries*, a collection of historic documents with commentaries (London: Burns & Oates, 1954), pp. 173—180.

[40] Mirbt, *Quellen*, No. 491, pp. 348, 349; Ehler and Morrall, *Church and State*, pp. 180—183.

[41] Ludwig von Pastor, *History of the Popes, from the Close of the Middle Ages* (London: Kegan Paul, Trench, Trubner & Co., Ltd., 1928), XVI, 218—223; Pollen, *Engl. Catholics in the Reign of Eliz.*, pp. 67 ff;

124

The pope might well make a gesture of good will toward Elizabeth, for she had shown a measure of good will toward some of the adherents of Rome. Among these were the monks and nuns. Parliament had passed "An Act to annex to the Crown certain religious houses and monasteries and to reform certain abuses in chantries."[42] The Spanish ambassador, Count de Feria, on leaving the country, had received permission from Elizabeth to take with him some of these religious, particularly the Carthusians and the Bridgettines of Syon. The Benedictines and the Dominicans, too, were forced to leave England; some of the Franciscans remained in England as an unorganized group.[43]

The attitude and the actions of the English government toward the regular clergy were more considerate than they were toward the secular clergy, especially the bishops. The deprivations of the bishops and of some of the clergy followed. None of them was executed for his refusal to take the oath of supremacy. Some of them were imprisoned. Edmund Bonner, bishop of London, was the first to be deprived of his office (30 May 1559). Immediately, or almost immediately, he was imprisoned in the Marshalsea, where he remained for the rest of his life; he died in 1569. Some of the

A. O. Meyer, *Engl. and the Cath. Ch. under Eliz.*, pp. 40 ff.; *Cambr. Mod. Hist.*, II, 578—581. J. H. Blunt, *The Reformation of the Church in England, Its History, Principles, and Results* (London: Rivingtons, 1882), II, 429 f, quoted the letter which Pius IV wrote, asking Elizabeth to return to the bosom of the church.

[42] 1 Elizabeth, cap. 24, Prothero, *Select Statutes*, pp. 37 f.

[43] Peter Guilday, *The English Catholic Refugees on the Continent, 1558—1795* (London: Longmans, Green & Co., 1920), I, 4 f; 41—58; 377, 378. Birt, *Eliz. Rel. Settlement*, pp. 213, 127—129, 135, 136.
Baron Caspar Breuner to the Emperor Ferdinand, London, 6 Aug. 1559, *Queen Elizabeth and Some Foreigners*, ed. von Klarwill, p. 108.
Il Schifanoya to Vivaldino, London, 2 May 1559, *Ven. Cal.*, VII (1558—80), No. 68, p. 79.
The Bishop of Aquila to Philip II, London, 19 June 1559: "The cloistered clergy here *(religiosos)* have all license to go and have already begun to depart." *Span. Cal., Eliz.*, I (1558—67), No. 36, p. 77.
Il Schifanoya to Vivaldino, London, 30 May 1559, wrote that this was a special request by Feria to Queen Elizabeth as a parting gift. *Ven. Cal.*, VII (1558—80), No. 77, p. 93.
Machyn's Diary, 4 July 1559, p. 204.

bishops were placed under custody. Bishop Tunstal was committed to Matthew Parker; death came to him before the year was out. Thirlby, also in Parker's custody, lived there ten years; Oglethorpe and Bayne both died in 1559. Turberville and Poole were given liberty. Scot, Goldwell, and Pate fled to the Continent. Nicholas Heath, the archbishop of York, too, was deprived of his office. After a short period in prison he was permitted to live in his own house, "quietly and nobly," said Strype, "yet giving security not to interrupt the laws of church or state, or meddle with the affairs of the realm." [44]

Several of these bishops, in December 1559, petitioned the queen to return to the Church of Rome. Mary had extinguished schisms and heresies, they said; Elizabeth's advisers, they intimated, had misled her. They wanted these advisers to repent of their heresies.[45] To ask the queen to acknowledge the supremacy of the Church of Rome was not, in their opinion, an act of disloyalty. Elizabeth answered them, taunting them with their past behavior:

And as for our father [Henry VIII] being withdrawn from the *supremacy* of Rome by schismatical and heretical counsels and advisers; who, we pray, advised him more, or flattered him, than you, good Mr. Hethe, when you were bishop of Rochester? And than you, Mr. Bonner, when you were archdeacon? And you, Mr. Turberville? Nay further, who was more an adviser to our father, than your great Stephen Gardiner, when he lived? Are not yet then those schismatics and heretics? If so, suspend your evil censures.

This, however, was not the whole answer. Her answer also warned them not to interfere in the Religious Settlement. "We give you warning, that for the future we hear no more of this kind, lest you provoke us to execute those penalties enacted for the punishing of our resisters: which out of our clemency we have forbore." [46]

[44] Strype, *Elizabeth*, I, i, 212; cf. pp. 207—216.

[45] Ibid., I, i, 217.

[46] Ibid., I, i, 218, 219; G. B. Harrison, ed. *The Letters of Queen Elizabeth* (London: Cassell and Co., Ltd., 1935), p. 30.

For the most part there was little opposition to the Religious Settlement. Many of the Romanists had gone along with the changes of the past twenty-five years, because of moderate policies. Moderation toward papists was recommended by Peter Martyr:

As touching the correction of the papists for things past, you must remember that punishments have been more than once discontinued for the sake of peace; and that an amnesty has sometimes been granted in the church, and that heretics have been received with their former honours and dignities, provided only that they should subscribe unto sound religion. Care however must be taken, . . . that in future they do nothing in opposition to the religion now received.[47]

There is no way of establishing with accuracy how many of the people of England in 1559 were in favor of the Religious Settlement, how many may have favored one part, e. g., the repudiation of the pope's supremacy or the liturgical changes, and not the other, how many believed that no change should have been made, or for that matter, how many were of the opinion that the change was not radical enough. The clergy were concerned about the doctrinal changes and the repudiation of the supremacy of Rome. The laity were less concerned about doctrine than liturgy, and the idea of separation from the supremacy of Rome was not foreign to them.[48] Early in Elizabeth's reign one observer remarked: "It is really very surprising to witness the very great fortitude of many persons, both bishops, lay-lords, and plebeians, who have not bowed the knee before Baal, and who are prepared to suffer any extreme punishment, rather than return to their former state under King Henry." [49]

[47] Peter Martyr to [Thomas Sampson]. Zurich, 1 Feb. 1560, *Zurich Letters,* II (1558—1602), II, No. XVII, p. 40.

[48] Hughes, *Reformation in England,* III, 48—95, has the best recent sympathetic treatment. I reached the conclusion that between 3 and 5 per cent of the population in England in 1559 might be called staunch Roman Catholic, in my "The Old Religion in England During the Reign of Queen Elizabeth (1558—70)," Unpublished Bachelor of Divinity Thesis, Concordia Seminary, St. Louis, 1930, pp. 84, 85.

[49] London, 6 Feb. 1559, *Ven. Cal.,* VII (1558—80), No. 19, p. 28.

There was no large exodus of fearful Romanists at the outset of Elizabeth's reign, such as there had been of Protestants in 1553, when Mary came to the throne. The number of Englishmen living in exile because of their religion grew in time. Eventually some of them plotted against the queen. In 1559, however, there were no traitors among them, and no one advocated rebellion.[50] Perhaps the unsettled conditions on the Continent accounted for this in part; perhaps some of the stauncher Romanists were practicing their faith without molestation. Pollard conjectured: "Often the same priest read the Anglican service in public to satisfy the law and then said mass in secret to satisfy his conscience."[51] Jewel, however, noted: "Now that religion is everywhere changed, the mass-priests absent themselves altogether from public worship, as if it were the greatest impiety to have anything in common with the people of God."[52] From these, no doubt, came the "hedge priests," as they later were called, some Marian priests who were deprived but who continued to serve Roman Catholics surreptitiously. Many masses, it was reported, were still being said, even in London, months after the adjournment of Parliament and the visitation of the commission.[53] To estimate how many of the priests there were, where they labored and to what extent, is impossible. We are told that

[50] Guilday, *Engl. Cath. Refugees,* I, 7—11; A. O. Meyer, *Engl. and the Cath. Ch. under Eliz.,* p. 35.

Bishop Quadra reported to Philip II from London, 27 June 1559: "The news is that in the neighbourhood of Winchester they have refused to receive the church service book, . . . No mass was being said, whereat the congregations were greatly disturbed." *Span. Cal., Eliz.,* I (1558—67), No. 39, p. 79. No overt rebellious action followed, however. A few days later he wrote to the king again, London, 1 July 1559: "They say that the Queen has news of religious disturbances in the North Country where they refuse to receive the new church services. I know for certain that in the diocese of Winchester they have not received it and will not take the oath, and that all is in confusion. They dare not press them." *Ibid.,* No. 41, p. 82.

[51] A. F. Pollard, *Political History* (1547—1603), p. 280.

[52] John Jewel to Peter Martyr, London, 1 Aug. 1559, *Zurich Letters,* I (1558—79), No. 16, p. 39.

[53] Bishop Quadra to Count de Feria, London, Jan. 1560, *Span. Cal., Eliz.,* I (1558—67), No. 84, p. 122.

128

in 1596, more than thirty-five years after the Religious Settlement, there were between forty and fifty of the old Marian clergy still active in England.[54] These men were forced to do their work in secret; for the most part the government allowed them to go their way unmolested; and the majority of them were never even arrested. The laws were strengthened in 1563 and in 1587 and in 1595, but in the early years of the reign of Elizabeth I the Romanists could gradually adjust themselves to the Religious Settlement. Most of them seem to have done that.

During this early period the Roman Catholics were virtually deserted by Rome; Peter was sleeping.

> No doubt the long history of the sufferings of English catholics comprised periods of much greater oppression than the first twelve years of Elizabeth, but at no other period did catholics see themselves so utterly forsaken by the church, or so entirely cut off from all communication with Rome, as at this period — especially in the seven years between the close of the Council of Trent and the queen's excommunication. . . . Numerous statements in support of this view are found in the reports of the Spanish ambassador.[55]

Among the followers of Rome, as among the Protestants during the reign of Mary, some drew the distinction between participation in a church service or mass, whichever the case might be, and merely being present. Others entered the church service after it had begun and left before it had been completed. Some attended the English service without apostasy, they believed, so long as they did not participate in Holy Communion. Some participated in the Sacrament, eating what they called "Calvin's profaned bread," because they disallowed its sacramental character.[56]

How many may have been turned from the Old Religion by the preaching of the reformers or even the reading of the *Homilies* no one would hazard to say. The *Homilies* repudiated the authority

---

[54] Birt, *Eliz. Rel. Settlement,* p. 301, with reference to William Holt, S. J., who made this statement in that year.

[55] A. O. Meyer, *Engl. and the Cath. Ch. under Eliz.,* p. 67.

[56] Ibid., p. 69.

of the bishop of Rome and the claims of the Roman Church to be the true church. They inveighed against some of the ceremonies and practices of that church. One sample of the polemics of the *Homilies* against the Old Religion may be noted:

> The true church is an universal congregation or fellowship of God's faithful and elect people, built upon the foundation of the apostles and prophets, Jesus Christ himself being the head cornerstone. And it hath always three notes or marks, whereby it is known: pure and sound doctrine, the sacraments ministered according to Christ's whole institution, and the right use of ecclesiastical discipline. . . . Now if ye will compare this with the church of Rome, not as it was in the beginning, but as it is presently, and hath been for the space of nine hundred years and odd, you shall well perceive the state thereof to be so far wide from the nature of the true church, that nothing can be more. For neither are they built on the foundation of the apostles and prophets, retaining the sound and pure doctrine of Christ Jesu: neither yet do they order the sacraments or else the ecclesiastical keys, in such sort as he did first institute and ordain them: but have so intermingled their own traditions and inventions, by chopping and changing, by adding and plucking away, that now they seem to be converted into a new guise.[57]

The differences in doctrine between the canons and decrees of the Council of Trent, completed in 1563, and the Thirty-Nine Articles, drafted in 1562, were known only to a few, and those few were theologians and scholars. Popular preaching pointed up some of the more obvious differences. Outward allegiance too often, it may be feared, was all that mattered to some Romanists and some Anglicans. The Old Religion was never suppressed in England, either in doctrine or in adherents. The steadfastness of the Romanists persisted.[58]

[57] *Certain Sermons or Homilies Appointed to be Read in Churches in the Time of Queen Elizabeth,* 3d American, from the last English ed. (Philadelphia: Edward C. Biddle, 1844), p. 414.

[58] Bishop Quadra to the Duke of Alva, London, 12 Nov. 1559, *Span. Cal., Eliz.,* I (1558—67), No. 73, p. 111, "Steadfast as saints," he said to Count de Feria, London, Jan. 1560, ibid., No. 84, p. 122.

CHAPTER VIII

PURITANISM AND THE ELIZABETHAN
SETTLEMENT

he terms "Puritan" or "Puritanism" were not used in 1559. They did not come into use until 1567 to 1568, during the days of the Elizabethan Vestiarian Controversy.[1] The Puritan party, nevertheless, existed already in November 1558, when Elizabeth came to the throne. The Puritans called themselves gospellers; they spoke of "our party." Instead of a highly formal organization informal relationships bound them close together. They did not think of themselves, nor did they wish to be regarded, as a faction either within the civil or the ecclesiastical order. The terms "Puritans," "Puritanism," and "Puritan faction" will, nevertheless, be used. Some convenient label must be found for that group of people who held decided views about the "cleansing" of the church of rites and ceremonies and usages which they regarded as distinctly Roman or popish, about the make-up of a Christian congregation, or about the polity of the church.

Puritanism had multiple roots. Some of them went back into the medieval church. In the Middle Ages those that disliked certain ceremonies and rites were not always labeled heretics. Occasionally small groups separated from this church; others remained within the church at least nominally. The followers of Wyclif, the Lollards, were forebears of Puritanism if that term is given a broad

---

[1] M. M. Knappen, *Tudor Puritanism: A Chapter in the History of Idealism* (Chicago: University of Chicago Press, 1939), p. 488.

meaning. The Lollard Conclusions of 1394 had "Puritan" over-tones.[2] The Christian Brethren, the "just, fast men," of the reign of Henry VIII prepared the ground for the germination and vigorous growth of the Puritan movement.[3] Even the Cambridge Group, the "Germans" that met at the White Horse Inn in the 1520s, by their active opposition to Romanism encouraged a theology of protest, based on the writings of the first of the Protestants, Martin Luther.

William Tyndale has been called the first Puritan.[4] His covenant theology may have been borrowed from Henry Bullinger in Zurich. Bullinger contributed more than any other individual Continental divine to the early growth of Puritanism.

Three Johns, John Bradford, John Hooper, and John Knox, active in England before the reign of Mary, established important aspects of the Puritan platform that were developed during the reign of Elizabeth.

John Bradford was the least important of the three Johns. Before his ordination as deacon by Nicholas Ridley he scrupled at the ceremonies. This was in 1550, just at the time when Hooper's

[2] Gee and Hardy, *Documents,* No. XLI, pp. 126—132. See Eri B. Hulbert, *The English Reformation and Puritanism* (Chicago: University of Chicago Press, 1908), pp. 41—51.

[3] Rupp, *Making of the English Protestant Tradition,* pp. 1—14.

[4] M. M. Knappen, "William Tindale — First English Puritan," *Church History,* V (September 1936), 201—215.

See also Paul R. Rust, *The First of the Puritans and The Book of Common Prayer* (Milwaukee: Bruce Publishing Co., 1949), p. vii et passim, who regards Cranmer, Ridley, Hooper, Latimer, and the other Protestants of this time as the "first of the Puritans." He did not single out Tyndale, however.

See also Leonard J. Trinterud, "The Origins of Puritanism," *Church History,* XX (March 1951), pp. 37—57. He says (p. 38): "Puritanism emerged in Tudor England in the thought and work of men such as William Tyndale, John Frith, John Bale, John Hooper, John Bradford, and their associates."

William Haller, *The Rise of Puritanism: Or, The Way to the New Jerusalem As Set Forth in Pulpit and Press from Thomas Cartwright to John Lilburne and John Milton, 1570—1643* (Harper Torchbooks; New York: Harper & Bros., 1957), is not greatly concerned about the origins of Puritanism. He does find, p. 5, that its roots go back far into the Middle Ages.

controversy about vestments was at its height.[5] However, his emphasis on preaching makes John Bradford a forerunner of later Puritan emphases. He was bold and audacious in denouncing the authorities for their slowness or failure in carrying out a more rapid and thorough "cleansing" of the church. John Knox in his *A Godly Letter sent too the fayethfull in London, Newcastle, Barwyke, &c* (printed in July 1554) said of him: "And Master Bradford (whom God for Christ's, His Son's, sake comfort to the end) spared not the proudest of them, but boldly declared, that God's vengeance shortly should strike those that then were in authority, because they loathed and abhorred the true Word of the everlasting God. . . ."[6] One of Bradford's letters was addressed to the Earls of Arundel, Darby, Shrewsbury, and Pembroke, "declaring the nature of the Spaniards and discovering the most detestable treasons, which they have pretended most falsely against our most noble Kingdom of England." To it was appended a poem written by an unknown author (designated simply as T. E.) and called "a tragical blast of the papistical trumpet for maintenance of the Pope's Kingdom in England."[7] The letter, with its appendix, showed that Bradford embodied hatred of the Roman religion, intense distrust of the Spaniards, a fervent patriotism, a zeal for ridding the church of abuses, and an extremely high regard for preaching. In all of these he was a Puritan before the Elizabethan era, one who laid down the lines which some of the later Puritans, in part, followed.

To him the mass was entirely idolatrous, and even in the days of the Marian persecution he would not agree that "any [could] be present at the mass in bodily presence, in spirit being absent," without offense to God. *The Hvrte of Hering Masse,*[8] in which

[5] Knappen, *Tudor Puritanism,* Appendix I, pp. 483—486.

[6] Quoted by S. R. Maitland, *The Reformation in England* (London: John Lane, 1906), p. 68.

[7] Ibid., pp. 122—124.

[8] John Bradford, "The Hurt of Hearing Mass," *The Writings of John Bradford, Containing Letters, Treatises, Remains,* edited for the Parker Society by Aubrey Townsend (Cambridge: The University Press, 1853), pp. 297—315.

these views were explained, was circulated widely. During those years, even while he was in prison, he quietly took over a position of leadership among the religious prisoners and their followers. His letters reached many with spiritual advice. Even Latimer, Ridley, and Cranmer were exhorted by him as by one who could write with definite assurance.[9]

Bradford spoke of God's covenant, but the concept was not prominent in his writings. More prominent was his teaching on predestination, or election. Here he taught the election to salvation; those who are lost, he taught, are lost by their own fault.[10] This was not the Calvinistic doctrine but the Lutheran. Only in this respect must his influence on later Puritanism be discounted, for Puritanism followed the Calvinistic teachings on predestination.

John Hooper is more easily recognizable as a pre-Puritan than John Bradford, for he was in the center of the controversy about vestments in King Edward's reign. Ridley defined the controversy in saying: "But all our controversy is this, whether the vestments as they be now appointed by the authority of the church of England be things lawful to be used, or may be used without the breach of God's law; that is, whether they be things as of themselves indifferent, and not forbidden as sin against God's holy word or no." [11] References to angels and the saints had to be omitted from the Oath of Supremacy before he would take this oath. He served as bishop of Gloucester and then of Worcester. Like John Bradford he suffered martyrdom during the reign of Queen Mary. Hooper wrote *A Godly Confession and Protestation of the Christian Faith* and *A Brief and Clear Confession of the Christian Faith*. This second confession was made up of a hundred articles. The 58th article

[9] See, e. g., his "Address on Constancy," in *The Writings of John Bradford, Containing Sermons, Meditations, Examinations,* edited for the Parker Society by Aubrey Townsend (Cambridge: The University Press, 1848), pp. 385—388.

[10] "Defence of Election," ibid., pp. 307—330.

[11] "Reply of Bishop Ridley to Bishop Hooper on the Vestment Controversy, 1550," *Bradford's Writings: Letters, Treatises, Remains,* p. 375, cf. pp. 375—395.

stated, in part, ". . . the Christian liberty of the gospel . . . doth deliver our consciences from all outward beggarly ceremonies by man ordained and devised without the word of God." [12] And in the 83d article, he wrote:

I believe also that the forbidding of marriage for certain persons, likewise the forbidding of certain meats, the difference of days, garments, and such-like, is the devilish doctrine of Antichrist, and wholly against the Christian liberty of the gospel taught by Jesus Christ, the which delivereth us from all outward ceremonies of the law, and setteth us at liberty to use all things with giving God thanks, so that it be not done to the hurt of our neighbour. For all things were made holy by the word of God and prayer to him that knoweth and receiveth truth. Therefore to compel the Christian to these things is but to take from them and to rob them of their Christian liberty, and by tyranny to set them under the curse of the law, from the which Christ by His death and passion hath delivered them: and it is one true mark and note to know Antichrist by. [13]

Hooper has little to say about the covenant. His position on predestination, or election, is Lutheran, or catholic, rather than Calvinistic. Again he shows that the early Puritans or the pre-Puritans did not have all the same doctrinal emphases that the Puritans at the time of Whitgift had. Regarding election — and the references he has are few — he wrote:

The cause of rejection or damnation is sin in man; which will not hear, neither receive the promise of the gospel; or else, after he hath received it, by accustomed doing of ill he fall either into a contempt of the gospel, will not study to live thereafter, or else hateth the gospel, because it condemneth his ungodly life. . . . The cause of our election is the mercy of God in Christ, Rom. ix. Howbeit, he that will be partaker of this election must receive

[12] *Later Writings of Bishop Hooper together with His Letters and Other Pieces,* edited for the Parker Society by Charles Nevinson (Cambridge: The University Press, 1852), p. 45.

[13] Ibid., pp. 55, 56.

the promise in Christ by faith. For therefore we be elected, because afterward we are made the members of Christ, Eph. i. Rom. viii.[14]

John Knox had perhaps an even greater influence on the English Puritans than did John Hooper or John Bradford. John Knox was in England between 1549 and 1553. For eighteen months he had served as a galley slave on a French vessel, a captive of war. When released, he did not dare to return to his native Scotland, where the Reformation had not yet been legalized. His stay at Berwick and then at Newcastle, before he became one of the six royal chaplains, helped him to perfect himself as a preacher and to gain a wider acquaintance with the progress of the Reformation in England than he had had before.

Knox's influence became evident in the "Black Rubric," appended to the Second Edwardian Book of Common Prayer. Knox had objected to the rubric (direction) which called for the reception of the Lord's Supper in a kneeling posture. The "Black Rubric" declared that the action in question did not imply any belief in the doctrine of transubstantiation. Kneeling was thus not to be interpreted in any way as demanding adoration of the host. Knox challenged the moderate position of Cranmer in the *Forty-Two Articles,* which declared ceremonies to be a matter of indifference. The article was dropped in Cranmer's version, a concession to harmony rather than an endorsement of extreme views. Cranmer's position here agreed with Luther's; Knox's position agreed with that of the later Puritans.

Knox was offered an English bishopric in 1552, but he refused it. Perhaps he wished to maintain his public forum in order to influence policy; perhaps he disliked the episcopal system. At any rate, on either count, Knox was acting in keeping with later Puritan policies. The Puritans had no time for bishops but ample time to preach to politicians and political leaders and to lend guidance to the state.

During the reign of Queen Mary, Knox was on the Continent

[14] "A Declaration of the Ten Holy Commandments of Almighty God," *Early Writings of John Hooper,* edited for the Parker Society by Samuel Carr (Cambridge: The University Press, 1843), p. 264.

most of the time. Here his *Faythful Admonition . . . to the Professours of God's Truthe in England*[15] was written. His return to Scotland in 1559 meant that his direct interference in English religious affairs was greatly minimized. Before 1559, however, he exerted a very direct influence among the refugees in Frankfort and Geneva. The "troubles at Frankfort" were due in part to Knox. His objections to the use of the Prayer Book brought on revisions of the liturgy, a few of which remained in effect even after Knox was forced to leave the city.

Although Puritanism suffered a setback in Frankfort, it gained strength in Calvin's Geneva. Here was published *The Forme of Prayers and Ministration of the Sacraments, etc., Used in the English Congregation at Geneva and Approved by the Famous and Godly Learned Man, John Calvin.*[16] It definitely decried the popish remains in the Edwardian Reformation. It would retain only that which was "within the compass of God's Word, which our Saviour hath left unto us as only sufficient to govern all our actions by; so that what so ever is added to this Word by man's devise, seem it never so good, holy, or beautiful, yet before our God which is jealous and can not admit any companion or counsellor, it is evil, wicked, and abominable."

When Elizabeth came to the throne, Knox was ready to rally the Puritans in exile; with him was a group of associates. But Knox's influence was not strong enough to coalesce the eager repatriates into a coalition that could bargain collectively with the new queen. His *Brief Exhortation* to England[17] received less notice than it deserved; he himself was not granted permission to enter England.

Knox's views on ceremonies and his *Genevan Service Book* had important consequences for the development of Tudor Puritanism.

[15] *S.T.C.* 15069 (See Chap. 1, fn. 16). See also William M'Gavin, *The History of the Reformation in Scotland* by John Knox, 4th ed. (Glasgow: Glackie & Son, 1844), pp. 409—442.

[16] *S.T.C.,* 16561.

[17] *S.T.C.,* 15073.
See also his *An Admonition or vvarning, S.T.C.* 15059. I have used the only known copy of this work (in the Folger Shakespeare Library, Washington, D.C.).

His views on "discipline" and church polity had even greater influence. His influence on men like Richard Cartwright and Walter Travers is self-evidently difficult to measure. That his views coincided with Calvin's does not make Knox simply an echo of the Genevan reformer. The dour Scot was independent enough, whatever the degree of dependence might seem to be.[18]

There were others besides Knox, Hooper, and Bradford — or even perhaps Tyndale and those among the exiles — who must be counted as the forerunners of the Elizabethan Puritans. During the period of the Marian persecutions there were secret congregations, perforce independent, in London, in Colchester, and even in the North. The congregation in London, at least, without a fixed meeting place, had an organization; pastors and deacons and possibly elders were found among them. Among their pastors Thomas Bentham must be singled out, "the bravest of the brave," to repeat a tribute paid to him.[19]

Among the *émigrés,* especially among those in Geneva, there developed doctrinal emphases that had been absent in a Hooper or a Bradford. Here Whittingham translated a work which bore the title *Beza: His Briefe Declaracion of the Chiefe Poyntes of Christian Religion, Set Forth in a Table of Predestination.* Here in the same year (1556) appeared Anthony Gilby's *A Briefe Treatice of Election and Reprobation with Certain Answers to the Objections of the Adversaries to This Doctrine.* Among them, too, appeared various tracts and brochures on political science, propagandistic bits aimed against Mary.[20] In Geneva, not in London, the theories and the practices of Puritan political policies evolved.

In Geneva, too, there appeared first an English translation of the New Testament and then the translation of the entire Bible. The New Testament appeared in 1557, "diligently revised by the most approved Greek examples, and conference of translations in other

[18] Geddes MacGregor, *The Thundering Scot: A Portrait of John Knox* (Philadelphia: The Westminster Press, 1957), has given an especially readable and trustworthy account of Knox.

[19] Knappen, *Tudor Puritanism,* p. 161.

[20] Ibid., p. 144.

tongues." This English New Testament, the first to be divided into verses, was the work of William Whittingham, who had sided with John Knox in the troubles at Frankfort. After the New Testament had been issued he busied himself with the Psalter, which was published in 1559. In that year most of the English exiles had returned home or were returning home; Whittingham remained behind in Geneva to complete the Geneva Bible, published in 1560. That Miles Coverdale, Thomas Sampson, and Anthony Gilbey had a hand in the translation and editing of the Geneva Bible is probable, but the burden of the work rested on Whittingham.

The Geneva Bible was based on the translation by William Tyndale, whose New Testament was put into print in 1525. Tyndale had also translated portions of the Old Testament. His work had been based on the Greek, not without use, however, of Luther's translation. Myles Coverdale completed the Tyndale translation of the Scriptures. Another revision, known as the Great Bible, appeared in 1539; it was reissued in the following year with a preface by Thomas Cranmer and is known as Cranmer's Bible. There had also appeared French translations by Pierre Robert Olivétan and Jacques Lefèvre d'Étaples. Whittingham used these as well as the previous English translations. This statement in no wise detracts from the scholarship of Whittingham. His translation is known as the Genevan Bible or the "Breeches Bible" (because Gen. 3:7 is rendered, "they . . . made themselves breeches"). The marginal notes and comments were decidedly Calvinistic in their point of view. The Genevan Bible shaped Puritan thought during the next fifty years and longer because of these annotations. The title included these words: "With moste profitable annotations upon all the harde places, and other things of great importance . . ." They were significant, almost as significant as the Sacred Scriptures themselves, to generations of Puritans.[21]

Another book, whose influence was to be second only to that of the Geneva Bible among the Puritans, was in the making during these same years. The *Book of Martyrs,* or the *Acts and Monu-*

[21] See especially Charles C. Butterworth, *The Literary Lineage of the King James Bible,* 1340—1611 (Philadelphia: University of Pennsylvania Press, 1941).

ments, by John Foxe, had been issued in its first edition in 1554, but Foxe was busy collecting materials for the second edition, in English, which was published in 1563. From Basle in May 1559 he had written: "I am here harassed to the utmost of my strength, and almost beyond my strength, in collecting the histories of the Martyrs. . . . I am more immediately concerned with British history, yet I shall not pass over the sacred history of other nations, should it come in my way." [22] His strength endured, and during his lifetime four editions of his work were published. Foxe was a partisan; his history is not without error. However, it cannot be dismissed simply as a piece of propaganda. His documents are valuable, and his facts are substantially correct. Generations of English Puritans, and American Puritans, too, knew few books beyond the Bible and Foxe.[23]

John Foxe may have been the author, in 1559, of a tract in Latin, *Ad Christum anglorum exultantium* εὐχαριστικόν. It strikes an intensely patriotic note in its thanksgiving for the opportunity to return to England. Praise to God is expressed because "those sharp flames of persecution, which otherwise no floods could put out," had been quenched. Only in generalities are the hopes expressed that the change in religion would come about, that pastors and people would have a regard for the truth, or that learning and meekness would bring about a better mind and obedience.

John Foxe also wrote another tract, a letter of congratulations to Queen Elizabeth on her accession, in the name of Germany. In it he pleaded that she would restore the light of the Gospel in the liberty "from base idolatry, false worship, manifest impiety, and forced dissimulation.[24]

The dedication of the Psalms, published in Geneva in 1559, also had the purpose of instructing Elizabeth. It compared her to the Queen of Sheba, pleading that she be zealous for the glory of God and ready to obey God's will, "diligent to suppress all papistry, vice, and heresy, and to cause the light of God's holy

[22] John Foxe to Henry Bullinger, Basle, 13 May 1559, *Zurich Letters,* I (1558—79), No. X, pp. 25, 26.

[23] Knappen, *Tudor Puritanism,* pp. 494 f.

[24] Strype, *Elizabeth,* I, i, 158—161.

word speedily to shine through all her dominions." Pointedly she was reminded that God would bless her if she "advanced His kingdom." [25] That kingdom, it was implied, was to be based on a Puritan ideology.[26]

The Puritan hopes at the outset of Elizabeth's reign may be gauged by a letter written to the queen from Zurich in January 1559. Many good men were saying, the letter stated, "that your majesty is seriously thinking of purifying the church and restoring religion." It reminded her (as the Puritans said time and time again) that kings should be the nursing fathers of the church and queens her nursing mothers. Two things were important, "first, that every reformation of the church and of religion be conducted agreeably to the word of God; and next, that no opportunity be afforded to any among your councillors, whose endeavours are tending to that object, either to hinder this most holy and of all things most necessary work, or at least to persuade you that it should be deferred." Any compromise or "unhappy compound of popery and the gospel" was to be avoided. The reformation of the church should be in entire agreement with the Word of God. The writer of this letter could not stress this point too strongly, and in that he was bringing a Puritan emphasis. Old garments and old leathern bottles, he said, using the Scriptural metaphors, were not patched with new cloth or filled with new wine; ". . . we assuredly know it to be impossible ever to consult the peace of the churches, or the purity of religion, so long as any relics of superstition are retained." In His kindness God had raised her up, he reminded Elizabeth, to complete the work begun by her pious brother. Assuredly, he implied, she knew that Edward's reformation had not gone far enough, and she also knew that no time was to be wasted in beginning her reformation. "This is the desire of all godly persons." [27]

All godly persons, this same scribe wrote to the Earl of Bedford,

[25] Ibid., I, i, 163—165.

[26] Knappen's treatment of Puritanism as idealism still maintains its position of superiority.

[27] Rudolph Gualter to Queen Elizabeth, Zurich, 16 Jan. 1559, *Zurich Letters,* II (1558—1602), No. III, pp. 3—8.

were congratulating England on the accession of Elizabeth, "by whose zeal it is universally hoped that true religion will be restored." To the queen's physician, Richard Masters, he also made a direct plea that the queen's reformation be thorough, not "of a mixed, uncertain, and doubtful character," not having in it the "seeds of popery." To him "the cause of the reviving church" was most dear. It need not be supposed that the Protestants on the Continent, especially in Zurich and Geneva, were more eager for a "thorough" reformation than the returning exiles. These shared the sentiment of "the faithful." [28]

The returned exiles had their representation in the first Elizabeth Parliament, a political faction, as has been shown. Sir Anthony Cooke and Sir Francis Knollys were two important and influential members of this Parliament. There was a "vital core of at least twelve and probably sixteen returned exiles in the House; possibly more." Sixty-four other members of the House of Commons "might, with due caution, be reckoned with the radical core." A hundred or more, if the full membership list were available, might be found in this "Protestant nucleus." There is evidence "of an organized movement operating through the House of Commons, the object of which was to force upon Elizabeth and her government a complete Protestant programme, at least as radical as that achieved by the close of Edward VI's reign." However, it was a more conservative settlement than they had wished. They did force modifications on Elizabeth in the compromise on the Prayer Book.[29] The "Puritan" activities explain the reference in the closing speech in this session of Parliament by Sir Nicholas Bacon to factions and sects and the warning against extremists.

Before this Parliament was adjourned, and while the discussions were rife regarding the Religious Settlement, the Westminster Disputation was held between certain bishops and some Protestant — may they be called Puritan? — theologians. It was held in the Parliament House, and the House of Commons attended. It was not an academic disputation such as the Leipzig Debate

[28] Rudolph Gualter to Lord Francis, Zurich, 16 Jan. 1559, ibid., No. IV, pp. 8—11.

[29] Neale, *E. & Parl.*, I, 33—84. *Vide supra* chs. I and II.

between Luther and Eck. Rather it reminds us of similar disputations before town councils in the Swiss cities, and it is a minor indication of the influence of the Swiss religious pattern on the Puritan faction. More important, however, it is an indication of the thinking of the Puritan divines, who believed that the godly clergy should instruct the officers of the state in their religious duties as magistrates. The election sermons of Puritan ministers in Massachusetts were cut from the same cloth. This point of view came from Calvin and Geneva, whereas Elizabeth's view of the relation of the church to the state was Melanchthonian, even Erastian.

Three questions were proposed which were to be answered in writing by each side, the written briefs becoming the oral presentations. The questions were:

Whether it was not against the Word of God, and the custom of the ancient church, to use a tongue unknown to the people, in the common prayers and the administration of the Sacraments?

2. Whether every church had not authority to appoint, change, and take away, ceremonies, and ecclesiastical rites, so the same were done to edification.

3. Whether it could be proved by the Word of God, that in the Mass there was a propitiatory sacrifice for the dead, and for the living? [30]

Dean Cole presented the arguments for the bishops on 31 March 1559 after some questions of procedure. The brief took up the first question and defended the use of the Latin language in the services of the church. The authority of the church was cited as a basis for its use: "Since the Church of Rome had appointed the Latin service to be everywhere used, it was schismatical to separate from it." [31]

The Protestants or Puritans had appointed Robert Horne to read their brief. They, self-evidently, adopted the affirmative: "It is against the Word of God, and the custom of the primitive church, to use a tongue unknown to the people in common prayers, and

[30] Strype, *Elizabeth,* I, i, 131, 134. Burnet, *Hist. of the Ref.,* 3d ed., pt. II, book iii, no. 3, pp. 254—256.

[31] See ibid., no. 4, pp. 258—263.

143

administration of the Sacraments." 1 Cor. 14 was adduced to show that all that is done in the church should be done for edifying, that nothing is to be spoken to the people of the congregation in an unknown tongue unless it is interpreted, that it is an absurdity to use an unknown tongue, and that it is not a common prayer if the people are not able to give their assent to it by saying Amen. It was not allowed that the use of the Latin language should be counted as a "thing indifferent." Other reasons "gathered out of the Scripture, and otherwise," were adduced. Justin Martyr and the liturgies of Basil and Chrysostom were cited as proof that the primitive church used "vulgar tongues" in its public services. Satisfied that the affirmative had been fully substantiated, they concluded: "Wherefore it is to be marveled at, not only how such an untruth and abuse crept, at the first into the church, but also how it is maintained so stiffly at this day; and upon what ground, these that will be thought guides and pastors of Christ's church, are so loath to return to the first original of St. Paul's doctrine, and the practice of the primitive catholic church of Christ." [32]

When the disputation was resumed after the weekend, an unscheduled dispute about procedures broke up the conference. The blame has been placed on the side of the bishops for the failure to carry on the debate in the prescribed manner, but it must be admitted that they had everything to lose and little to gain. They maintained that Roman Catholic doctrine had already been established and ought to be debated only in a synod of theologians. Heretics were encouraged by discoursing before the unlearned multitude. Two of the bishops, the bishops of Winchester and of Lincoln, even said that the queen and the council deserved excommunication for arranging the disputation, a remark that earned for them a term in the Tower. The official report of the members of the council gave contempt and obstinate disobedience as the causes for the arrest and imprisonment. [33]

[32] Strype, *Elizabeth*, I, ii, 465—487, no. xv, "Dr. Horne's preface to his discourse, read at the conference at Westminster Abbey," and no. xvi, "The Protestants' discourse, prepared to have been read in the public conference at Westminster, upon the second question."

[33] Burnet, *Hist. of the Ref.*, 3d ed., pt. II, book iii, no. 5, pp. 263—265.

This official report was printed and disseminated. John Jewel wrote a long letter to Peter Martyr in Zurich, telling him about the disputation. When they gathered at Westminster on the 31st of March, he said, "Great were the expectations of the people, and the crowd, I believe, still greater." The victory on that first day belonged to the reformers, he said. "The debate was at length concluded in such a manner, that there was hardly any one in the whole assembly, not even the Earl of Shrewsbury, who did not adjudge that day's victory to be on our side." The altercations of the 3d of April were detrimental to the Romanists, he wrote. "It is altogether incredible, how much this conduct has lessened the opinion that the people entertained of the bishops; for they all begin to suspect they refused to say anything only because they had not anything to say." It was a useless conference, he judged.[34] Not so Richard Cox. He — to judge by a letter to one of his friends — regarded the rout of the Romanists as a decisive step in the re-establishment of Protestantism. "The sincere religion of Christ is therefore established among us in all parts of the kingdom, just in the same manner as it was formerly promulgated under our Edward, of most blessed memory."[35]

The discourse which the Protestants had prepared for this disputation on the second question brings some of the main viewpoints of the Puritans. The point dealt with rites and ceremonies. "By ceremonies and rites of the church," they said, "we understand those ceremonies and rites, which neither expressly, neither by necessary deduction or consequence, are commanded or forbidden in the Scripture, but are things of their own nature indifferent." These ecclesiastical rites and ceremonies were instituted for order and decency in the church. Again 1 Cor. 14 was used as the basis for their arguments. The words of Christ "Wheresoever two or three are gathered together in My name, there am I in the midst of them" (Matt. 18) were adduced to show that

[34] John Jewel to Peter Martyr, London, 6 April 1559, *Zurich Letters,* I (1558—67), No. V, pp. 13—17.

[35] Richard Cox to Wolfgang Weidner, London, 20 May 1559, ibid., No. XI, pp. 26—28.

churches have the right to change ceremonies and usages. Obedience to Christ and His Word are required of any and all churches who would change, alter, abrogate, or add to the rites and ceremonies, it was argued; abuses can creep in, and so useful ceremonies can become harmful. Every particular church ought to have the right, therefore, to make changes in such ceremonies. General councils meet too seldom to expect that corrections can come only through them. The seven churches in Asia Minor were given the mandate to correct their abuses by St. John (see the Book of Revelation). The same authority is given to all pastors in kingdoms and provinces today, they said. If this right were lacking, the churches would be obligated to obey men rather than God. "Therefore a particular church is not bound to retain, but may remove hurtful ceremonies, instituted by men." All of these reasons, numbered under six points, were taken out of the Scriptures, according to their brief; next they would proceed to find sanction out of the ancient writers and practices of the primitive church. These arguments are brought "to match them with their own weapons" in the debate. For the Protestants the arguments from Scripture would be enough. Nevertheless they adduce also two arguments from natural reason. "But reason would that things should be restored by like order as they fell in decay." Corruption begins in a particular place, and so it is reasonable that reformation should belong to a particular place. It is reasonable, too, to assume that where there is authority to begin there is authority to terminate. Diversities of ceremonies were advocated, for in that way the liberty of the church remains and ceremonies are not esteemed as equal with the Word of God.

These reformers asserted that the argument that the bishop of Rome is the head of the universal church was not germane to the question under discussion. They only hinted as to the nature of their objection, since now they wished to establish the general principle that rites and ceremonies may be altered. They wrote:

Moreover, the late experience within this our country doth declare, that the abrogation of many ceremonies established by general authority is lawful and profitable. For in the time of King Henry

146

VIII of famous memory, many superstitions and idolatrous rites were abolished; and by the consent of many of them which now are, and of late have been, adversaries; as pilgrimages, stations, pardons, many superstitious opinions of purgatory, holy water, of masses for cattle, and *scala coeli,* innumerable lies out of the church legends, of feigned miracles, and saints lives.[36]

After Parliament had enacted the settlement, dissatisfaction was expressed by the Puritan faction. "The doctrine is every where most pure; but as to ceremonies and maskings there is a little too much foolery," John Jewel wrote to Peter Martyr. Then he continued: "That little silver cross, of ill-omened origin, still maintains its place in the queen's chapel." [37] Another was so troubled in his conscience that he wrote to Peter Martyr to learn from him what to do about the misery that hung over them, as he expressed it. His letter epitomized the problem which the Puritans faced, as it summarized their misgivings, and may therefore be quoted at length by way of conclusion. The letter was written on 6 Jan. 1560.

I have now been in England one year, and that not a quiet one; but I fear that the year now coming on will only bring me yet more trouble. I am not however the only one who am afraid for myself, but we are all of us in fear for ourselves; yet I dare not commit to writing the evils that seem to be hanging over us. I implore you . . . to pray God most earnestly on our behalf. Contend for this, for this I say, that the truth of the gospel may be neither obscured nor overturned in England.

These were the misgivings of a large group. The consecrations ("as we call it") of some of the new bishops were decried. This was a genuine Puritan attitude. He exclaimed:

O my father, what can I hope for, when the ministry of the word is banished from court? while the crucifix is allowed, with lights burning before it? The altars indeed are removed and images also throughout the kingdom; the crucifix and candles retained at court alone. . . . What can I hope, when three of our lately ap-

---

[36] Strype, *Elizabeth,* I, ii, 466—485, no. xvi; I, i, 133—138.

[37] John Jewel to Peter Martyr, London, 16 Nov. 1559, *Zurich Letters,* I (1558—67), No. XXIV, p. 55.

pointed bishops are to officiate at the table of the Lord, one as priest, another as deacon, and a third as subdeacon, before the image of the crucifix, or at least not far from it, with candles, and habited in the golden vestments of the papacy; and are thus to celebrate the Lord's Supper without any sermon? What hope is there of any good, when our party are disposed to look for religion in those dumb remnants of idolatry, and not from the preaching of the lively word of God? [38]

These were searching questions which troubled the Puritans throughout the reign of Elizabeth and into that of the Stuarts.

The "heads of the misery that is hanging over us" were not recognized by all. The Elizabethan Settlement had not gone far enough to remove them for the Puritans.

In April 1559, it seems, the divines of the Puritan faction determined that they ought to present a confession of faith in a defense against the charges that they were heretics and "that we are fallen from the doctrine of Christ's catholic church." They were especially concerned about protesting their loyalty to Elizabeth, stating that the Word of God did not disallow the rule of women and that rebellion by private persons was against that same Word of God.[39] In an oration delivered to Queen Elizabeth at the beginning of her reign, it was stated that "malicious Mary," had caused the children of "our natural mother England" to suffer under her tyranny. "Virtuous Elizabeth" was therefore exhorted:

The realm will soon be purged, if vice and self-love be utterly condemned. It will be in good state preserved, if these three things — God's word truly taught and preached, youth well brought up in godly and honest exercises, and justice rightly ministered — may be perfectly constituted. . . . Wherefore, for God's sake, noble queen, let not the opportunity, now by God offered, be by your grace omitted.[40]

Puritanism and patriotism were joined with loyalty to Elizabeth.

[38] Thomas Sampson to Peter Martyr, 6 Jan. 1560, ibid., No. XXVII, pp. 62—65.

[39] Strype, *Elizabeth,* I, i, 166—173.

[40] Foxe, *Acts and Monuments,* ed. Cattley, VIII, 673—679.

CHAPTER IX

THE THIRTY-NINE ARTICLES

In the sixteenth century, men demanded clear-cut statements of doctrine. The Lutherans had presented their confession to the Emperor Charles V at the Diet of Augsburg in 1530. At the same time Huldrich Zwingli of Zurich had readied his *Ratio fidei;* Martin Butzer, too, wanted to present a confession of the four cities. These, however, did not receive the recognition which the Lutheran *Augsburg Confession* received. Attempts at reconciliation between the Lutherans and the Romanists failed, largely because of adherence to doctrinal tenets. Even the attempts to bring about a political alliance between Henry VIII of England and the German Protestant princes of the Schmalkald League failed, partly because the Lutheran political leaders demanded subscription to their confession by the English king.

The year which saw the settlement of the religious issue in England witnessed the formulation of the *Gallic Confession,* a statement of the beliefs of the Huguenot church. The year after the Elizabethan Settlement John Knox brought about the adoption of the *Confessio Scoticana.* This was followed in the next year in the Lowlands by the drafting of the *Belgic Confession.* Three summaries of Calvinistic doctrine in three countries, 1559 in France, 1560 in Scotland, 1561 in the Netherlands, set a pattern that could not be ignored in England, even if religious leaders there had wished to do so. These three came in the wake of the final revision of John Calvin's *Institutes of the Christian Religion* in 1559, the thirty-four-year-long avocation of the Genevan reformer.

The Romanists, too, were intent on formulating their doctrinal beliefs. The Council of Trent had met from 13 Dec. 1545 to 11 March 1547, again in 1551 and 1552, and for a third assembly from 18 Jan. 1562 to 4 Dec. 1563. Before the end of the following month, on 26 Jan. 1564, Pope Pius IV confirmed the proceedings of the council. Almost immediately the College of Cardinals compiled the *Profession of the Tridentine Faith* in twelve articles or, as it is also called, the *Creed of Pius IV*. Roman Catholic doctrine had been fixed on systematic lines.

In England, it is true, some formulations of doctrine had already been made. During the reign of Henry VIII the negotiations between the German Lutherans and the English produced the *Ten Articles* and the *Thirteen Articles,* neither of official standing or of a comprehensive nature. The *Bishop's Book,* or the *Institution of a Christian Man,* was a confession of faith tending toward Protestantism. Later came the *King's Book* or the *Necessary Doctrine and Erudition for Any Christian Man.* In the meanwhile, however, Parliament had interposed the *Six Articles.* All of these formulations preceded the *Forty-Two Articles,* which became the basis for the *Thirty-Nine Articles.*[1]

The original title of the *Ten Articles* tells much of the purpose of this first formal statement of doctrine drawn up for the Church of England, *Articles to stablyshe christen quietnes and unitie amonge us, and to avoyde contentious opinions.* The articles themselves contained, in the words of the preface, doctrines "such as be commanded expressly by God, and be necessary to our salvation" and those which contributed to "a decent order and honest policy." The authority of the Sacred Scriptures and the ancient creeds was asserted. The traditional teaching on Baptism was affirmed, and the sacrament of penance was taught. They called for "a certain

---

[1] Hardwick, *History of the Articles of Religion,* pp. 39—114; Henry E. Jacobs, *The Lutheran Movement in England During the Reigns of Henry VIII, and Edward VI, and Its Literary Monuments: A study in Comparative Symbolics* (Philadelphia: General Council Publication House, 1916), pp. 339—342; Rupp, *Making of the Engl. Prot. Tradition,* pp. 128 to 154; Strype, *Elizabeth,* I, i, 484—488.

faith, trust, and confidence of the mercy and goodness of God, whereby the penitent must conceive certain hope and faith that God will forgive him his sins, and repute him justified, and of the number of His elect children, not for the worthiness of any merit or work done by the penitent, but for the only merits of the blood and passion of our Saviour Jesu Christ." This sacrifice of Christ was regarded as sufficient in the sight of God for the remission of all sins to all sinners and the eternal punishment of their sins. The doctrine here set forth was distinctly Lutheran. Justification is due to the "only mercy and grace of the Father, promised freely unto us for His Son's sake Jesu Christ, and the merits of His blood and passion." This did not exclude the necessity of good works; "God necessarily requireth of us to do good works commanded by Him." This was good Lutheran doctrine. Also the article on "The Sacrament of the Altar" set forth the doctrine of the Real Presence. There may be a question whether this article taught the Roman doctrine of transubstantiation when it stated: ". . . under the same form and figure of bread and wine the very selfsame body and blood of Christ is corporally, really, and in the very substance exhibited, distributed, and received unto and of all them which receive the said sacrament." Other articles dealt with religious practices, such as images, honoring the saints, praying to saints, of rites and ceremonies, and of purgatory. The last article was almost equivocal and bore the stamp of compromise. This first formulation of doctrine in 1536, the *Ten Articles,* must be regarded of prime importance for future formulations.[2]

The godly and pious Institution of a Christian Man (1537) has the subtitle, "the exposition or interpretation of the common creed, of the seven Sacraments, of the ten commandments, and of the Pater Noster and the Ave Maria, Justification and Purgatory." Justification was again set forth in accord with the teachings of Martin Luther. Even the addition of the four further sacraments of the Roman Church did not altogether meet the approval of those who wished to be loyal to Rome. On the Eucharist the

[2] Hardwick, *History of the Articles of Religion,* Appendix No. 1, pp. 231—248; Burnet, *Hist. of the Ref.,* Part I, book iii, pp. 236—244.

teaching of the *Ten Articles* was repeated. The volume was as much an exposition as a formulation.[3]

Its influence was more decisive than the influence of the *Thirteen Articles*. These articles of 1538 were not put into print until the nineteenth century. Whatever purpose they served in shaping the thinking of Thomas Cranmer and other English theologians, they were not recognized by king or clergy in general. Their significance, however, in the development of English doctrinal formulations ought not to be minimized. Nor should their Lutheran ancestry be discounted. Verbal similarities are not simply accidental; the literal identity of five of the thirteen articles with the corresponding articles of the *Augsburg Confession* has been established; the heavy dependence of the remaining articles on the *Wittenberg Articles*, likewise, has been acknowledged. Their use by Cranmer while writing the *Forty-Two Articles* establishes their importance.[4]

However, the action of Parliament in 1539, in adopting the *Six Articles,* constituted a reversal in the doctrinal developments within England.[5] Whatever the purpose of this legislation might have been in the mind of Henry VIII, it served to keep theological trends under the control of the monarch. Perhaps it showed that theological considerations were to serve nationalistic interests or at least the interests of Henry VIII.

The title of the theological exposition known as the *King's Book* of 1543 emphasized the same consideration: *A Necessary Doctrine and Erudition for any Christian Man: set forth by the King's Majesty of England.*[6] On justification and on free will the Lutheran doctrines were not taught. This was a trend away from the Protestantism of the period from 1536 to 1538. Henry VIII was not ready to espouse the teachings of his former opponent, Martin Luther, even though he himself repudiated the power and the

[3] Hughes, *Reformation in England,* II, 30—37.

[4] Hardwick, *History of the Articles of Religion,* Appendix No. 2, pp. 249—263.

[5] Gee and Hardy, *Documents,* No. LXV, pp. 303—319.

[6] Hughes, *Reformation in England,* III, 46—58.

authority of the Bishop of Rome. The earlier attempts to formulate doctrinal statements awaited the death of Henry VIII for their fulfillment.

This fulfillment came with the formulation of the *Forty-Two Articles*.[7] Their wording was almost entirely the work of Thomas Cranmer, whose Lutheran proclivities became evident especially during the early years of the reign of Edward VI. The *Forty-Two Articles* were published late in the reign of this king, so that their importance is greater in relationship to the revisions made in the reign of Elizabeth I than in the use made of them in 1552 and 1553. An analysis, article by article, would therefore contribute comparatively little to an understanding of the *Thirty-Nine Articles*.

The *Thirty-Nine Articles* were not published immediately in 1559. To further unity of doctrine in this critical period, Matthew Parker drew up the *Eleven Articles* in 1559. Subscription to them was to be, too, a testimony of the common consent of the Elizabethan clergy to this doctrine. The document dealt with some of the main topics of the Christian religion. Belief in the Trinity was affirmed; the Scriptures, it was acknowledged, contain "all things necessary to salvation," and the three ecumenical creeds were accepted. The church was given three marks: the true teaching of the Word of God, the orderly administration of the Sacraments, and the use of the authority of the keys. "Every such particular church hath authority to institute, to change, clean to put away ceremonies, and other ecclesiastical rites, as they be superfluous, or be abused, and to constitute other making more seemliness, to order, or edification," Article III stated in line with the proposition set forth at the Westminster Disputation. The queen's prerogatives and supremacy were acknowledged; the bishop of Rome was repudiated. The Book of Common Prayer as set forth

---

[7] "Articles Agreed upon by the Bishops, and other Learned and Godly Men, in the Last Convocation at London, in the year of our Lord, 1552, to root out the discord of opinions, and establish the Agreement of true Religion, published by the Kings Majesties Authority, 1553," *Collection of Articles*, pp. 39—52 (English), pp. 53—64 (Latin); Hardwick, *History of the Articles of Religion*, Appendix No. 3, pp. 265—323 (Articles of 1552, 1562, and 1572).

by the Parliament of 1559 was endorsed. Paragraphs on Baptism, the Holy Supper, and the call of the minister of the Word were included. Images were disparaged, and works of mercy and charity were extolled.[8]

The *Eleven Articles* are dependent on the *Forty-Two Articles*, but only in part. They give evidence of the influence of the Puritan divines on the thinking of Matthew Parker. Their place in the development of the *Thirty-Nine Articles* and their authority may be told in the words of Hardwick:

> It does not appear that this Formulary had been put in circulation by the authority of the royal council; and as the houses of Convocation did not assemble until the year 1562, it was destitute of all ecclesiastical sanction, excepting so far as the consent of the bishops involved the acquiescence of the lower clergy. Issuing, however, as it did, from the press of the Queen's printer, and being enforced by episcopal injunctions upon the whole body of incumbents, it claims to be regarded as a public manifesto, and as an authentic record of the teaching of the Church through the interval which elapsed from the time of its appearance to the revival of the longer Articles in the ensuing Convocation.[9]

It was not until the year 1562 that this convocation issued the first revision of the *Forty-Two Articles*.[10] In 1571 subscription to them was required by a canon of Convocation and by an enactment of Parliament. They are, nevertheless, an integral part of the Elizabethan Settlement and the statement of the doctrinal position of the then Church of England.

The Lutheran sources for the *Forty-Two Articles* and, in turn, for the *Thirty-Nine Articles,* can readily be identified. The *Augsburg Confession* contributed words, phrases, paragraphs, and inter-

[8] Hardwick, *History of the Articles of Religion,* Appendix No. 4, pp. 325—329.

[9] Ibid., pp. 120, 121.

[10] "Articles Agreed upon by the Archbishops and Bishops of Both Provinces and the Whole Clergy, in the Convocation Holden at London, in the year 1562, for the avoidance of diversities of opinions, and for the establishing of Consent touching True Religion," *Collection of Articles,* pp. 87—109; Hardwick, loc. cit.

pretations to at least one third, or thirteen, of the *Thirty-Nine Articles.* Seven more of the articles were definitely influenced in their phraseology by the *Wuertemburg Confession,* or the *Apology of the Augsburg Confession,* or both; in one instance, at least, there is reason to believe that the *Schmalkald Articles* were used. This is not to say that the authors or compilers of these articles lacked independence in theological judgment or acumen. They found these prototypes expressing their deliberate opinions and beliefs, and they did not hesitate to identify themselves with these reformers by using the language of their confessional statements. Philip Melanchthon had been the chief author of the Lutheran confessions which Cranmer, and after him Parker, used in writing the English articles. Even Henry VIII had had a kindlier regard for Melanchthon than for Luther. The recognition of much that is Lutheran in the *Thirty-Nine Articles* is a recognition of the catholicism of sixteenth-century Lutheranism and Anglicanism alike.[11]

The first five articles dealt with the Godhead. They affirmed belief in the Trinity in conformity with the ancient Apostolic, Nicene, and Athanasian creeds. This Godhead is a unity, "of one substance, power, and eternity, the Father, the Son, and the Holy Ghost." [12] Deniers of the Trinity were scarce in the England of Elizabeth. On the Continent, it is to be remembered, a Servetus approximated Sabellianism. The later Unitarians of Poland, subscribers to the *Cracow Catechism,* denied the deity of both the Son and the Spirit. The followers of Socinus joined these Unitarians. In their own *Racovian Catechism,* making much of a rationalistic argument, they taught that the Second Person of the Godhead was not true God but mere man.

The emphatic statement therefore on the incarnation of the Son of God affirmed alike the humanity of the Logos and the deity of

---

[11] See my "Cranmer's Legacy," *Concordia Theological Monthly,* XXVII (April 1956), 263—268 and the references cited there.

Rogers' *Thirty-Nine Articles,* p. vi, cited the 1585 title of his work as *The English Creed; consisting with the true, ancient Catholic and Apostolic Church in all the Points and Articles of Religion, etc.*

[12] Article I

the Son of man. "The Godhead and Manhood were joined together in one Person, never to be divided, whereof is one Christ, very God and very man." [13] No detailed statement with an enumeration by name of ancient heresies was made. The refutation of those heresies was inherent in the very phrases that were used. Christ's suffering, sacrifice, and propitiation were affirmed. "As Christ died for us, and was buried; so also it is to be believed that He went down into Hell." [14] Controversies regarding this doctrine were raging. The article of 1552 had stated: "The body lay in the sepulchre until the resurrection, but His ghost, departing from Him, was with the ghosts that were in prison or in hell, and did preach to the same, as the place of St. Peter doth testify." [15] Neither version, however, was really helpful in settling disputed points then. On the resurrection of Christ there was ample clarity. He "did truly arise again from the death, and took again His body." And as He rose again from the dead, as also the ancient creeds confessed, so He ascended into heaven. There, it was taught, He "sitteth, until He returns to judge all men at the last day." [16] The resurrection, ascension, session, and return of the Son of God are asserted. The work of the God-man was "to reconcile His Father to us," for He "died for us." The substitutionary, or vicarious, purpose of the incarnation was affirmed. Nor were the mysteries of any doctrines allowed to obscure this basic teaching of catholic Protestantism and the Scriptures.

The article dealing with the Holy Spirit was added by Archbishop Parker from the Lutheran *Wuertemburg Confession.* Perhaps this article was added in order to make the presentation on the Godhead complete; perhaps the revival of some ancient heresies was feared. The article was completely orthodox in the Western tradition, for it taught the procession of the Spirit from the Father and the Son. The distinction between the three Persons in the Godhead was implied, although the three are of the same sub-

[13] Article II.
[14] Article III.
[15] *Collection of Articles,* p. 41.
[16] Article IV.

156

stance. The deity of the Holy Spirit was stated, for He was called "very and eternal God." [17] No distinctive doctrine for that day was emphasized in this article. The affinity between Anglicanism and Lutheranism was recognizable by anyone who knew the Lutheran prototype of this article; the affinity of Protestantism of the sixteenth century with the teachings of the ancient church, too, was evident to anyone who would study the fathers of the early church and the Scriptures.

The Scriptures had to be the ultimate norm and authority for the Protestant reformers, since they repudiated the authority of the bishop of Rome. The sufficiency of the Holy Scriptures for salvation, and specifically the Old Testament, formed the subject of two articles.

Holy Scripture containeth all things necessary to salvation; so that whatsoever is not read therein, nor may be proved thereby, is not to be required of any man that it should be believed as an Article of the Faith, or be thought requisite or necessary to salvation. [18]

This article evidently placed the Church of England in the camp of Protestantism on the principle of *sola Scriptura,* Scripture alone, the principle so dear to the heart of Martin Luther. The reliance of the church of Rome on tradition, or the decrees of the popes or even of the councils, was not allowed. The Council of Trent in its first pronouncements already in 1546 had published a decree which coupled the written books of the Scriptures with the unwritten traditions. [19] The Romanists had thus shown that they regarded the Scriptures as insufficient. Not so the Anglicans. The "Homily on Holy Scripture," written by Thomas Cranmer, first in the *Book of Homilies,* has the following in its opening paragraph: "forasmuch as in it is contained God's true word, setting forth His glory, and also man's duty. And there is no truth nor

[17] Article V.

[18] Articles VI—VII.

[19] H. J. Schroeder, editor and translator, *Canons and Decrees of the Council of Trent,* original text with English translation (St. Louis: B. Herder Book Co., 1950), 29, Sess. vi, chs. i ff.

157

doctrine necessary for our justification, and everlasting salvation, but that is (or may be) drawn out of that fountain and well of truth."[20] The fathers concurred in their testimony as to the sufficiency of the Holy Scriptures, and the reformers of the conservative Reformation agreed. Among the Anabaptists there were those who stressed the illumination of the Spirit. Others distorted the meaning of the Old Testament and its relationship to the New. No agreement with them was voiced in the *Thirty-Nine Articles.* Radicals and Romanists alike were dismissed by a positive, simple, direct statement. That there might be no misunderstanding, there was given the list of books which composed the Sacred Scriptures or the canon.[21]

Again, that there might be no misunderstanding, the formularies of the ancient church are cited, and agreement with them was affirmed. The ecumenical creeds of Christendom, which "may be proved by most certain warrants of Holy Scripture," were named as those which "ought thoroughly to be received and believed."[22]

Four further articles among the thirty-nine dealt with the nature of man. Separate articles were devoted to original sin, free will, Christ's sinlessness, and sin after Baptism. The articles go back to the former righteousness which man had at his creation and now find a fault and corruption in his nature. Now he is very far gone from his original righteousness, inclined to evil, and deserving of God's wrath and damnation.[23] Only Christ is sinless; the Sin-Bearer is the sinless One.[24] Only in Him is grace given to man to turn from sin, "the grace of God by Christ preventing us," says the article in its archaic English, using the term "preventing" in its original meaning "coming beforehand." Monergism, to use the

[20] "A Fruitful Exhortation to the Reading and Knowledge of Holy Scriptures," *Sermons or Homilies Appointed to be Read in Churches in the Time of Queen Elizabeth,* new ed. (London: J. G. & F. Rivington, 1833), p. 1.

[21] Article VI.

[22] Article VIII.

[23] Article IX.

[24] Article XV.

158

language of the theologians, was affirmed; that means that man's conversion and faith and life of holiness are all totally the work of God alone. That man in any way in his conversion works together with God ("synergism") was entirely denied.[25] Man commits sin after his Baptism. A right understanding of God's grace, the article pointed out, in accord with the Scriptures, leads to a realization that the sinner who has fallen from grace may again by the grace of God be restored and amend his sinful life.[26] "Free will" had been the topic of the controversy between Erasmus and Luther. Erasmus was well known and admired in England. However, the teachings of Luther, not those of Erasmus, were followed by Cranmer and repeated by Parker, so that in the articles on free will and original sin a definite Lutheran ring was discernible. The *Augsburg Confession,* especially its second article, was close at hand when the English confession was drafted.

The Lutheran wording was evident, too, in the articles which deal with salvation. The article which speaks of the justification of man taught: "We are accounted righteous before God, only for the merit of our Lord and Saviour Jesus Christ by faith, and not for our own works or deservings." *Sola fide,* justification by faith, was called "a most wholesome doctrine, and very full of comfort." A reference was made to the "Homily of Justification." Since there is no "Homily on Justification," the reference is obviously to the "Homily of Salvation." [27] This homily, the third in the *Book of Homilies,* was also written by Thomas Cranmer. The opening paragraph of that homily read:

Because all men be sinners and offenders against God, and breakers of His law and commandments, therefore can no man by his own acts, works, and deeds (seem they never so good) be justified, and made righteous before God: but every man of necessity is constrained to seek for another righteousness or justification, to be received at God's own hands, that is to say,

[25] Article X.
[26] Article XVI.
[27] Article XI.

159

the forgiveness of his sins and trespasses, in such things as he has offended. And this justification or righteousness, which we so receive of God's mercy and Christ's merits, embraced by faith, is taken, accepted, and allowed of God, for our perfect and full justification. For the more full understanding hereof, it is our parts and duties ever to remember the great mercy of God, how that (all the world being wrapped in sin by breaking of the law) God sent His only Son our Saviour Christ into this world, to fulfil the law for us, and by shedding of His most precious blood, to make a sacrifice and satisfaction, or (as it may be called) amends to His Father for our sins, to assuage His wrath and indignation conceived against us for the same.[28]

Robert Barnes, "Luther's English friend," might have written that for Cranmer, or possibly William Tyndale, another man who had been at Wittenberg. Be that as it may, Cranmer was intent on showing his agreement with Scriptures, particularly with the apostle Paul. He cited various passages from Paul's letters and said:

In these foresaid places, the apostle toucheth specially three things, which must go together in our justification. Upon God's part, His great mercy and grace; upon Christ's part, justice, that is, the satisfaction of God's justice, or the price of our redemption, by the offering of His body, and shedding of His blood, and fulfilling the law perfectly and thoroughly; and upon our part, true and lively faith in the merits of Jesus Christ, which yet is not ours, but by God's working in us: so that in our justification, is not only God's mercy and grace, but also His justice, which the apostle calleth the justice of God, and it consisteth in paying our ransom and fulfilling of the Law: and so the grace of God doth not shut out the justice of God in our justification, but only shutteth out the justice of man, that is to say, the justice of our works, as to be merits of deserving our justification.[29]

[28] "A Sermon of the Salvation of Mankind, by Only Christ Our Saviour, from Sin and Death Everlasting," *Sermons or Homilies,* p. 19. See fn. 20.

[29] Ibid., pp. 20, 21.

Works, however, were not regarded as unnecessary. As fruits of faith they are evidences of a lively, living faith, pleasing and acceptable to God in Christ. For that reason works done before the individual has come to faith are not good works in the sight of God.[30] Nor can anyone assert that he has done works of supererogation, more than God requires; no one can render to God more than he is bound to render.[31]

However, the articles dealing with salvation would be incomplete, especially in the age of Calvin, without an article on predestination or election. The seventeenth article of the *Thirty-Nine Articles,* which has the caption "Of Predestination and Election," nonetheless, cannot be labeled "Calvinistic." It avoided entirely any teaching on double election or an election to reprobation. It followed closely the language of Scripture throughout. The similarity between the Latin wording of the Vulgate and the Latin wording of the article is very noticeable. Rom. 8:29-30, Rom. 9:11, and Eph. 1:3-11 are the chief passages from the Scriptures which were followed. Predestination to life was the keynote of the entire article. The comfort of this election in Christ was emphasized for those who know the workings of the Spirit of God. This doctrine is "full of sweet, pleasant, and unspeakable comfort to godly persons." It is not, the article implied, a horrible decree, as Calvin would have it. Perhaps Thomas Cranmer, who drew up the article originally, had been influenced in his concept of this doctrine by William Tyndale. Tyndale had been influenced by, and had used, Luther's preface to St. Paul's Epistle to the Romans. The Anglican article was very close to the Lutheran view. Other contemporaries and co-workers of Cranmer, such as good, old Hugh Latimer, the great preacher, held Cranmer's views. In spite of the controversies of that day, and particularly in spite of the formulations in the *Lambeth Articles* of 1595, or the *Canons of the Synod of Dort* of 1619, or the *Westminster Confession* of 1648, the *Thirty-Nine Articles* must be regarded as anti-Calvinistic. Article XVII was Lutheran, or, better still, Scriptural. It was in harmony with the

30 Article XII.

31 Article XIV.

catholicism of the early Christian Church. It was grounded, as the following article brought out, on the doctrine of salvation in Christ alone. "For holy Scripture doth set out unto us only the Name of Jesus Christ, whereby men must be saved." [32]

Those who believe in Christ Jesus come to Him through the ministrations of the church. That church is regarded as visible which has the pure teaching of God's Word and the right administration of the sacraments. The Eastern Church and the Roman Church have erred, the article declared, in matters both of ceremonies and of faith. The definition of the church was such that Anabaptist views are excluded. The Church of Rome's claim of being the only church was denied.[33] Nothing is said about the "invisible" church, a concept found among Calvinist theologians. Discipline is not made a mark of the church, in contrast to Puritan teachings regarding the church. Much has been read into this article by later Anglican divines. However, the following article on the authority of the church struck a balance between Puritan and Romanist views. It placed the authority of the church on the authority of the Word. "Wherefore," it said, "although the Church be a witness and a keeper of Holy Writ, yet, as it ought not to decree any thing against the same, so besides the same ought it not to enforce any thing to be believed for necessity of Salvation." [34] Even the decrees of general councils have "neither strength nor authority" unless they are in conformity with the Holy Scriptures. Such councils are to be convened by the princes — a curious concession to civic control, inconsistent with other clauses of this article.[35] Here was reflected a concern with the Council of Trent, which had not been convened by princes.

The anti-Roman concern was shown also in other articles. Those dealing with the traditions of the church,[36] the language to be used

[32] Article XVII.
[33] Article XIX.
[34] Article XX.
[35] Article XXI.
[36] Article XXXIV.

162

in church services,[37] and the marriage of the priests[38] opposed the teachings and practices of the Old Religion. God's Word, it was said, permits diversities of ceremonies and usages. Nationalism was made a prominent particle in the determination of the particular usages to be followed. Here was reflected the emphasis which politicians would give to the role of the church, although the churchmen would see to it that a final clause was added, "so that all things be done for edifying."[39] The catholic flavor of some of the previous articles was here abandoned.

No fault ought to be found, however, with the article that called for the public prayer and administration of the Sacrament in the language which the people would understand.

The article that permitted the marriage of priests was aimed, of course, at the practice of the Roman Church. Most of the prominent reformers of the sixteenth century, once they had broken with Rome, were married — among them Luther, Calvin, Zwingli, Butzer, and Cranmer.

Priests, or any man exercising the office of the ministry of the church, must be lawfully called. The *Augsburg Confession* had declared that "no one should publicly teach in the Church or administer the Sacraments unless he be regularly called."[40] Who is called lawfully? The Anglican article said: "And those we ought to judge lawfully called and sent, which be chosen and called to this work by men who have public authority given unto them in the Congregation, to call and send Ministers into the Lord's vineyard."[41] Nothing was said about proper ordination in the apostolic succession. The rites of the *Book of Consecration of Archbishops, and Ordering of Priests and Deacons,* adopted in 1548, are sufficient for a right, orderly, and lawful consecration.[42] There was neither a purely Lutheran nor, certainly, a Roman emphasis in these articles.

[37] Article XXIV.
[38] Article XXXII.
[39] Article XXXIV.
[40] *Augsburg Confession,* Article XIV.
[41] Article XXIII.
[42] Article XXXVI.

Later Anglican emphases, too, seem to be entirely lacking in the articles of 1562.

A number of other articles dealt with what might be called practical matters. One spoke "Of Excommunicated Persons How They Are to be Avoided."[43] Still another spoke "Of Christian Men's Goods, Which Are Not Common";[44] still another, "Of A Christian's Man's Oath."[45] These recognized the force of Anabaptist ideas in that day, an impact not always understood four centuries later. The article which spoke of the civil order may, too, have been directed against the Anabaptists in part. It intended chiefly, it must be admitted, to incorporate the state-church arrangement which had been set up by the Act of Supremacy, first in 1534 and then in 1559, into the official confession of faith. Royal supremacy is explained and defended, and all jurisdiction of the bishop of Rome is repudiated.[46] Eminently practical, too, especially for the priests or pastors, was the article which called for the use of the *Homilies,* both the first and the second book.[47] They were not popular with the Puritanical or Romanish clergy. The article which repudiated belief in purgatory may likewise be classed as a "practical" one, inasmuch as it denied a Roman Catholic doctrine.[48]

Six of the *Thirty-Nine Articles* deal in one way or another with the sacraments. The article which speaks of the sacraments in general received extensive revisions in 1562. The definition of a sacrament, however, was taken directly from the *Augsburg Confession,* in language which Cranmer had used in the *Forty-Two Articles.* The definition implied a disavowal of the definitions used by Zwingli, Calvin, and the Anabaptists. The number of sacraments is said to be two, not seven as taught by the Roman Church. Sacraments are ordained by Christ; they are more than tokens or

[43] Article XXXIII.
[44] Article XXXVIII.
[45] Article XXXIX.
[46] Article XXXI.
[47] Article XXXV.
[48] Article XXII.

164

signs. They are sure witnesses and effectual signs; by them God "doth work invisibly in us and doth not only quicken, but also strengthen and confirm our Faith in Him." According to this definition, the sacraments create spiritual life, nourish that life and make it strong, and add certainty to the certainty of faith. They are more than an aid to faith.[49] Although the article did not use the phrase, it taught that the sacraments are means of grace, media by which God's grace comes to men.

The efficacy of the sacraments, therefore, does not depend upon the worthiness of the officiant. In the church these means, the Sacrament and the Word, are dispensed, and the grace of God makes them effectual because of Christ's institution and promise. This does not mean that wicked ministers should be tolerated within the church. Their wickedness, however, does not take away from the valid use of the means of grace.[50]

Baptism, one of these means of grace, was called "a sign of regeneration or new birth." Infant Baptism was taught in opposition to the Anabaptists. The non-conformists who called themselves Baptists, whether General Baptists or Particular Baptists, were not yet in existence as a separate body. The article did not prescribe the mode of baptism. The promises of the forgiveness of sins and of the adoption to sonship in Christ Jesus are imparted through Baptism. Through Baptism the individual is made a member of the church; "they that receive baptism rightly are grafted into the Church." Every Baptism administered with water in the name of the Father and of the Son and of the Holy Ghost was considered a right Baptism. All they who are so baptized become members of one body in Christ and are united in the one holy catholic church.[51] The opening of the *Catechism* of the Church of England enjoined the confession that through Baptism the child is made a member of Christ.[52] This is in harmony with the teaching of the *Articles*.

---

[49] Article XXV.
[50] Article XXVI.
[51] Article XXVII.
[52] "A Catechism," *Two Liturgies,* p. 369.

The second sacrament, the Lord's Supper, was treated at greater length than the first. The article excluded the Roman Catholic teaching on transubstantiation, the Lutheran teaching of the Real Presence, the Zwinglian teaching of the purely symbolical character of the Sacrament, and the teachings of the Anabaptists, who would make it merely a love feast. The Lord's Supper was called "a Sacrament of our Redemption by Christ's death." A spiritual interpretation was given this sacrament. "The Body of Christ is given, taken, and eaten, in the Supper, only after an heavenly and spiritual manner. And the means whereby the Body of Christ is received and eaten in the Supper is Faith." [53] The wicked, therefore, do not eat the body of Christ in the use of the Lord's Supper.[54] The Roman custom of denying the cup to the laity was repudiated for the *sub utraque* of the primitive church.[55] The uniqueness and the all-sufficiency of the sacrifice of Christ on the cross were affirmed; the falsity of any view that made each mass a sacrifice independent of or additional to the sacrifice of the Cross was asserted. Christ died once for all. "The offering of Christ once made is the perfect redemption, propitiation, and satisfaction, for all the sins of the whole world, both original and actual, and there is none other satisfaction for sin but that alone." [56] Here the article was in harmony with the teachings of Luther and of the early church. Luther, however, would not have agreed with the teaching of the earlier article. This article denied, as Luther taught and as has been set forth in the translation of Jonas' *Catechism,* known as *Cranmer's Catechism,* that the body and blood of Christ is "in, with, and under the bread and the wine." [57] The *Thirty-Nine Articles*

[53] Article XXVIII.

[54] Article XXIX.

[55] Article XXX.

[56] Article XXXI.

[57] *A Short Instruction into Christian Religion,* being a Catechism set forth by Archbishop Cranmer in MDXLVIII: together with the same in Latin, translated from the German by Justus Jonas in MDXXXIX, ed. Edward Burton (Oxford: The University Press, 1829), Part I, p. 213. See my article, "Cranmer's Legacy," *Concordia Theological Monthly,* XXVII (April 1956), 254, 255.

followed the teachings of Martin Butzer and Peter Martyr, which were nearly akin to those of John Calvin. So close were the teachings of Butzer, Martyr, and Calvin that they can scarcely be distinguished.[58] Articles XXVIII and XXIX are "Calvinistic."

Only these two articles of the thirty-nine may genuinely be classified as belonging to the tradition of the Helvetic Reformation. All other articles are in the tradition of the Wittenberg Reformation, with the possible exception of Article XXXVII. Some of them were more ambiguous than similar articles in the Lutheran confessions. The influence of the *Augsburg Confession,* the *Apology,* and the *Wuertemburg Confession* was great.

Even more decisive, however, was the consciousness of a return to the teachings of the early church. The authority of the Scriptures was invoked repeatedly. The Scriptures were the norm and the authority for doctrine. The articles, too, consciously differentiated between the beliefs of the Church of Rome and those of the Church of England. No agreement was sought with the Anabaptists. The articles aimed at a broad basis for a national church within the framework of the conservative Reformation.

[58] McLelland, *The Visible Words of God,* Appendix C. But see Dugmore, *The Mass and the English Reformers,* pp. 221—247, who finds here "the Augustinian realist-symbolist tradition."

EPILOG

Elizabeth's "Puritan fanatics had no more obstinate opponent: she, in turn, had no more devoted worshippers. It is the strangest paradox of her reign and the supreme tribute to her greatness."[1] This statement epitomizes the role Elizabeth played in the religious settlement which bears her name. More is involved in this interpretation than simply the question of Tudor absolutism, or the personal monarchy of this queen, or the nationalism of fanatics who had eaten the bitter bread of exile. Included are the personal religious predilections of the queen, her political ideology, her domestic policy, and her guidance of foreign affairs.

The question of Elizabeth's personal religious convictions is almost as delicate as the question of her virginity. The circumstances of her mother's relations with her father compelled her, it is generally stated, to repudiate the authority of the bishop of Rome.[2] Her training, however, was a more decisive factor. In the personal policy of Elizabeth a desire for unity, a readiness to com-

[1] Sir John Neale, "The Via Media in Politics: A Historical Parallel," *Essays in Elizabethan History*, p. 124.

[2] Conyers Read, *Mr. Secretary Cecil and Queen Elizabeth*, p. 126: "She was of course by the fact of her birth as well as by her training and temper committed to the break with Rome."

Theodore Maynard, *Queen Elizabeth*, p. 67: "It is argued in all the Protestant histories that the circumstances of Elizabeth's birth, and therefore her title to the throne, necessitated the repudiation of the Pope's authority. This, however, is not the case. No Pope could, of course, have given an explicit acknowledgement of her legitimacy; but there was no inclination in Rome to raise that awkward issue."

169

promise, and a recognition of adiaphoristic principles are evident. Elizabeth's statecraft was colored by Melanchthonian theology.[3]

The traditional interpretation of the Elizabethan Settlement as a *via media* is not incorrect. The "middle way," however, was not simply a compromise between Puritanism and Romanism; it was also a philosophic and theological concept that owed something to Melanchthon, Starkey, and others because of Elizabeth.

Elizabeth's personal popularity was another factor in the settlement, for religio-patriotic sentiments were associated with her. They are evident in the "Deborah" or "Judith" cult and still more in the "Gloriana" cult of the Virgin Queen.[4]

At the very beginning of her reign Elizabeth had been advised to

> proceed to the reformation, having respect to quietness at home, the affairs you have in hand with foreign princes, the greatness of the Pope and how dangerous it is to make alteration in religion, especially in the beginning of a prince's reign. Glasses with small necks, if you pour into them any liquor suddenly or violently, will not be so filled, but refuse to receive the same that you would pour into them. Howbeit if you instil water into them by little and little they are soon replenished."[5]

Elizabeth was an expert at "pouring liquor," in her relationship with her own people and in her foreign relations.

Elizabeth's choice of Matthew Parker was her act of transferring spiritual authority into the hands of an official who would serve her with much the same outlook, ideology, and ideals that she herself possessed. Both believed in unity of doctrine, conformity in liturgical matters, moderation, and a readiness to serve the best interests of the nation. Melanchthonian adiaphoristic principles may have been part of Parker's political thinking.[6]

[3] W. Gordon Zeeveld, *Foundations of Tudor Policy*, pp. 128, 129; 136—145.

[4] See Maynard, pp. 314—317.

[5] Quoted by Read, *Elizabeth and Cecil*, pp. 127 f.

[6] See the delightful essay by Charles F. Mullett, "The Elizabethan Settlement and the Church," *Concordia Theological Monthly*, XXX (September 1959), 643—658.

However, the settlement was essentially the *Elizabethan* Settlement. A poem with the title "A Praise for Her Majesty's Most Gracious Government," which dates from late in her reign, demonstrates this point and summarizes what is meant by "Elizabeth I and the Religious Settlement of 1559."

Rejoice, O England blest!
Forget thee not to sing:
Sing out her praise, that brought thee rest
From God thy mighty King!

Our God and mighty King
Our comfort hath renew'd:
Elizabeth, our queen, did bring
His word with peace endu'd.

His word with peace and love
She planted, and it stands:
Her helper was the King above;
She brings it from his hands.

She brings it from his hand;
His counsel did decree,
That she, a Hester in this land,
Should set his children free.

None ruleth here but she;
Her heavenly guide doth shew,
How all things should decreed be
To comfort high and low.

Oh, sing then, high and low!
Give praise unto the King
That made her queen: none but a foe
But will her praises sing.

All praises let us sing
To King of Kings above!
Who sent Elizabeth to bring
So sweet a taste of love.[7]

[7] John Norden, *A Progress of Piety, Whose Jesses Lead into the Harbour of Heavenly Heart's Ease,* reprinted for the Parker Society (Cambridge: The University Press, 1847), pp. 44 f.

171

BIBLIOGRAPHICAL NOTE

The footnotes reflect much of the literature that has been used. The author has attempted to go back to original sources. Quotations from them have usually been modernized.

John Strype has been used extensively. Strype is poorly organized; he can be verbose; his interests are limited. However, he included many documents in his volumes. The publications of the Parker Society are of great value to the student of historical theology of this period. An extensive bibliography is provided by Conyers Read, whose *Bibliography of British History, Tudor Period, 1485—1603* (Oxford: The Clarendon Press, 1959) has now appeared in its second edition. The bibliography in J. B. Black's *The Reign of Elizabeth, 1558—1603* (Oxford: The Clarendon Press), first published in 1936 and now reprinted four times, is useful. The three-volume history of *The Reformation in England,* by Father Philip Hughes, published by The Macmillan Company, combs the literature of the period and provides many fruitful leads. Its bibliography might have been organized better.

Among older works those by A. O. Meyer, *England and the Catholic Church under Queen Elizabeth,* authorized and translated by J. R. McKee (London: Kegan Paul, Trench, Truebner & Co., Ltd., 1916); and Henry N. Birt, *The Elizabethan Religious Settlement* (London: George Bell and Sons, 1907), must be singled out. The former was written by a Lutheran; the latter, by a Roman Catholic. Meyer's study deals with only one aspect of the settlement, but it could not neglect the wider picture. Birt's study, also based on original sources, is not favorable to the Elizabethan Settlement.

Marshal Mason Knappen's *Tudor Puritanism* (University of Chicago Press, 1939) is still the best one-volume work on Puritanism.

Sir John Neale's works have been extremely helpful. His *Elizabeth I and Her Parliaments, 1559—1581* (New York: St. Martin's Press, 1958), contains three important chapters on the Parliament of 1559. *The Elizabethan House of Commons,* though an earlier work, is useful. His *Essays in Elizabethan History* (New York: St. Martin's Press, 1958) presents important insights into this period. His biography, *Queen Elizabeth I,* first published in 1934 and translated into eight languages, is available also in the Doubleday Anchor paperback edition.

Monographs and articles in learned journals are listed in Reade. This bibliographical notice serves mainly as an acknowledgment of the main sources used by the author.

INDEX

174

Bible 12, 107
  authority of 150, 157, 167
  daily reading of 57
  French translations of 139
  interpretation of 122
  sufficiency of 157, 158
  translation of 138, 139
Bibliography 173
Bibliography of British History, Tudor Period, Conyers Read 173
Bill for Making Ecclesiastical Laws by Thirty-Two Persons 53
Bilney, Thomas 78
BIRT, HENRY N. 120, 125, 129, 173, 174
BISHOP, EDMUND 61
Bishop of Chichester 50, 84, 113
Bishop of Coventry and Litchfield 52, 84
Bishop of London 50—52, 62, 84, 86, 89, 125
Bishop of Rochester 64, 113
Bishop of Winchester 50, 51, 84, 113, 144
Bishop's Book 150
Bishops 44, 48, 49, 75—77, 81 to 88, 125
BLACK, J. B. 92, 173
Black Rubric 62, 64, 136
Blaurer, Thomas 87
BLUNT, J. H. 125
Boleyn, Anne 3—6, 15, 27, 78
Bolingham, Nicholas 84
Bonner, Edmund 50, 51, 125, 126
Book of Common Prayer 11, 24, 32, 42, 46, 49, 57—73, 79, 81, 107, 136, 153
Book of Homilies 157, 159
Book of Martyrs, John Foxe 139
Both kinds 15, 24, 31, 32, 35, 99, 166
Boxoll, John 93
Bradford, John 132—134, 138
Brandenburg-Nurenberg Kirchenordnung 61
Breuner, Caspar 91

BREWER, J. S. 5
Bridgettines of Syon 125
Brief Exhortation, John Knox 137
BROWN, RAWDON 10
BRUCE, JOHN 77, 79—83, 89, 94
Bucer, Martin 6, 59, 78, 149, 163, 167
Bullinger, Henry 10, 21, 46, 86, 88, 91, 95, 132
Bulls 124
BURNET, GILBERT 27, 43, 143, 144, 151
Burnings 8, 31, 78
BURTON, EDWARD 166
BUTTERWORTH, CHARLES C. 6, 139

Calendar of Patent Rolls 92, 93
Calvin, John 78, 83, 129, 137, 138, 149, 161
Calvinism 6, 11, 24, 85, 86, 88, 90, 134, 135
Cambridge 7, 78, 79, 81, 132
Caraffa, Giovanni Piero, Paul IV 123, 124
Carlstadt 119
CARR, SAMUEL 136
Cartwright, Richard 138
Cassander, George 87
Cateau-Cambresis 36
Catechism 68, 69, 107, 119, 155, 165, 166
Catherine de Medici 8
Cecil, William 12, 17—20, 64, 80, 81, 91, 94
Ceremonies; *see* Rites and ceremonies
CHAPUYS 5
Charles I 3
Charles V 149
Charles, archduke of Austria 16
Cheney, Richard, Lutheran bishop 85
Chest for the poor 104, 105
Christian III 12
Christian Brethren 132
Chrysostom 65, 144

176

177

178

180

Protestantism 5, 6, 18, 24, 41, 54, 94, 111, 145
Protestants viii, 8, 13, 18, 28, 32, 34, 45, 46, 49, 88, 113, 120, 128, 142
PROTHERO, G. W. 14, 27—29, 31, 39, 44, 47, 48, 125
Proviso 45, 46
Prudence 13, 21
Psalter 59, 79, 139, 140
PULLAN, LEIGHTON 61
Purgatory 99, 123, 164
Puritans vii, 18, 30, 36, 41, 43, 45, 46, 55, 68, 69, 71, 75, 85, 87, 90, 95, 131—148, 169, 174
PURVIS, J. S. 105—108

Quadra, Alvarez de 18, 128, 130
Queen Elizabeth I, John Neale 174
Quignon 61

Racovian Catechism 155
Ratio fidei, Huldrich Zwingli 149
READ, CONYERS 19, 169, 170, 173
Readers 90
Real Presence 11, 12, 35, 60, 61, 63, 64, 85, 88, 119, 151, 166
REDGRAVE, G. R. 8, 15, 16
Reformatio legum ecclesiasticarum 53, 54
Reformation 9, 12, 13, 146
Reformation in England, Philip Hughes 173
Reformation Parliament 24
Regnans in excelsis, Pius V 124
Reign of Elizabeth, J. B. Black 173
Relics 109
Restitution of First Fruits and Tenths 28, 29, 39, 77
Revilers 24
Rich 47, 51
Ridley, Nicholas, Bishop of London 51, 52, 62, 119, 132, 134
Rites and ceremonies 14, 44—47, 57, 64, 65, 72, 73, 98, 99, 123, 130, 131, 135, 137, 143, 145 to 147, 151, 153

Robert, Lord Dudley 16
Rogers, Edward 18
ROGERS, THOMAS 110, 111, 155
Roman Catholic faith 9, 94, 113 to 130
Roman Catholicism 10, 11, 144; see also Old Religion
Roman rites 7, 11
Romanists 18, 34, 36, 41, 45, 50, 55, 88, 90, 113, 132, 145, 149
Rome 24, 28, 39, 76, 83, 91
ROWSE, A. L. 11, 85, 104, 110
RUPP, E. G. 78, 132, 150
RUST, PAUL R. 132

Sacrament of penance 150
Sacraments 90, 164, 165
SAMPSON, THOMAS 84, 85, 88, 139, 148
Sandys, Edwin 9, 10, 84, 87, 94, 110
Sarum liturgy 32, 59
Schoolmaster 106, 107
SCHROEDER, H. J. 157
Scory, John 82, 84, 87
Scot, Cuthbert 116—119, 126
Scotland 12, 136, 137
Scriptures; see Bible
Secretary 17, 18, 20, 94
Sermon 71, 112
Servetus 155
Seymore, Thomas 4
Shakespeare 5, 6
Simler, Josiah 86
Six Articles 150, 152
Smithfield fires 8
Socinus 155
SOUTHERN, A. C. 121
Spain 9, 12, 18, 24, 88, 133
STARKEY, THOMAS 6, 7, 170
Statecraft 7, 20, 21, 170
STEPHENS, H. MORSE 27, 28
Stokes, George, founder of Parker Society 79
STONE, J. M. 9
STRICKLAND, AGNES 9

181

STRYPE, JOHN 26, 64—67, 77, 79
to 82, 84, 85, 87, 90, 91, 99,
100, 102, 103, 109, 115—121,
123, 126, 140, 141, 143, 144,
147, 148, 150, 173
Succession 24, 27
Sunday observance 43, 48, 54
Supremum Caput 28, 37, 117
Sweden 12, 16

TANNER, J. R. 108
Ten Articles 150—152
Tensions 42, 43
Theodosius 119
Theological problems viii, 13, 20,
31
Theology of protest 132
Thirlby, Thomas 126
Thirteen Articles 150, 152
Thirty-Nine Articles 130, 149 to
169
Tigurine influence 7
Tithes 103
Title 27, 28, 31, 35, 37, 39, 115
Tower 7, 144
TOWNSEND, AUBREY 133, 134
Transubstantiation 11, 35, 63, 100,
114, 123, 136, 151, 166
Travers, Walter 138
Treason 7, 27, 28, 39, 133
TRINTERUD, LEONARD J. 132
Tudor Puritanism, Marshal Mason
Knappen 174
Tunstall, Cuthbert 81, 126
Turberville 126
Tyndale, William 132, 138, 139,
160, 161

Unitarians 155
Unity 26, 36, 45, 55, 56, 115, 116
Utenhovius 91
Utopia, Thomas More 20

Vacancies 75—78, 92, 113
Valentine 119
Vasa, Gustavus 12
VAUGHAN, RICHARD 79

Vestiarian Controversy 46, 131
Vestments 44, 62, 65, 66, 85, 102,
134
Via media 6, 30, 85, 170
Virginity 4, 17
Viscount Montague 34, 37, 47
Visitations 89, 92, 94, 97, 107 to
110
Vivaldino, Ottaviano 10, 13, 28,
29, 33, 35—37, 42
Vives, Juan Luis, tutor to Mary 5

Wales 76
WARE, SEDLEY L. 104
Watson, John 93
Welfare 20, 103, 104
Welsh Marches 19
Westminster Abbey 26, 98
Westminster Disputation 75, 120,
142—145, 153
White Horse Inn 78, 132
WHITEBROOK, J. C. 76, 82
Whitgift 135
Whittingham, William 138, 139
Wied, Herman von 59, 61
Witches 109
Wolsey 6, 18
Women, rule of 8, 15, 116, 148
Woodstock 7
Worship 32, 41, 143
Wotton, Nicholas 81
Writs of summons 26, 28
Wuertemburg Confession 155, 156,
167
Wyatt's uprising 7
Wyclif, John 16, 121, 131

Young, Thomas 84

ZEEVELD, W. GORDON 6, 170
ZUCK, LOWELL 7
Zurich 132
Zurich Letters 10, 14, 21, 23, 76,
84, 89, 91, 95, 109, 115, 127,
128, 140, 141, 145, 147
Zwingli, Huldrich 118, 119, 149
Zwinglianism 24, 63, 88, 91, 118

182